THE EARLY
STUART KINGS,
1603–1642

QUESTIONS AND ANALYSIS IN HISTORY

Edited by Stephen J. Lee, Sean Lang and Jocelyn Hunt

Other titles in this series:

Modern History

Imperial Germany, 1871–1918
Stephen J. Lee

The Weimar Republic
Stephen J. Lee

Hitler and Nazi Germany
Stephen J. Lee

The Spanish Civil War
Andrew Forrest

The Cold War
Bradley Lightbody

Stalin and the Soviet Union
Stephen J. Lee

Parliamentary Reform, 1785–1928
Sean Lang

British Foreign and Imperial Policy, 1865–1919
Graham D. Goodlad

The French Revolution
Jocelyn Hunt

The First World War
Ian C. Cawood and David McKinnon-Bell

Early Modern History

The English Wars and Republic, 1636–1660
Graham E. Seel

The Renaissance
Jocelyn Hunt

Tudor Government
T. A. Morris

Spain, 1474–1598
Jocelyn Hunt

The Early Stuart Kings, 1603–1642
Graham E. Seel and David L. Smith

THE EARLY STUART KINGS, 1603–1642

GRAHAM E. SEEL and
DAVID L. SMITH

ROUTLEDGE

London and New York

First published 2001
by Routledge
11 New Fetter Lane, London EC4P 4EE

Simultaneously published in the USA and Canada
by Routledge
29 West 35th Street, New York, NY 10001

Routledge is an imprint of the Taylor & Francis Group

Typeset in Akzidenz Grotesk and Perpetua by
Keystroke, Jacaranda Lodge, Wolverhampton
Printed and bound in Great Britain by
Biddles Ltd, Guildford and King's Lynn

British Library Cataloguing in Publication Data
A catalogue record for this book is available from the British Library

Library of Congress Cataloging in Publication Data
Seel, G. E. (Graham E.), 1963–
    The early Stuart kings, 1603–1642 / Graham E. Seel and David L. Smith.
    p. cm. – (Questions and analysis in history)
    Includes bibliographical references and index.
    1. Great Britain–History–Early Stuarts, 1603–1649. 2. Great Britain–
History–Early Stuarts, 1603–1649–Problems, exercises, etc. 3. Great
Britain–Kings and rulers–Biography–Problems, exercises, etc. 4. Great
Britain–Kings and rulers–Biography. I. Smith, David L. (David Lawrence),
1963– II. Title. III. Series.
DA390 .S44 2001
941.06′1–dc21   00-051709

ISBN 0–415–22400–4

For J. T. Bever

CONTENTS

SERIES PREFACE

Most history textbooks now aim to provide the student with interpretation, and many also cover the historiography of a topic. Some include a selection of sources.

So far, however, there have been few attempts to combine *all* the skills needed by the history student. Interpretation is usually found within an overall narrative framework and it is often difficult to separate the two for essay purposes. Where sources are included, there is rarely any guidance as to how to answer the questions on them.

The Questions and Analysis series is therefore based on the belief that another approach should be added to those which already exist. It has two main aims.

The first is to separate narrative from interpretation so that the latter is no longer diluted by the former. Most chapters start with a background narrative section containing essential information. This material is then used in a section focusing on analysis through a specific question. The main purpose of this is to help to tighten up essay technique.

The second aim is to provide a comprehensive range of sources for each of the issues covered. The questions are of the type which appear on examination papers, and some have worked answers to demonstrate the techniques required.

The chapters may be approached in different ways. The background narratives can be read first to provide an overall perspective, followed by the analyses and then the sources. The alternative method is to work through all the components of each chapter before going on to the next.

ACKNOWLEDGEMENTS

The authors and publishers are grateful to the following for permission to reproduce copyright material:

Cambridge University Press, for extracts from: Johann P. Sommerville (ed.), *King James VI and I: Political Writings* (1994); J. P. Kenyon (ed.), *The Stuart Constitution: Documents and Commentary* (2nd edition, 1986); Irene Carrier, *James VI and I: King of Great Britain* (1998); Christopher W. Daniels and John Morrill, *Charles I* (1988). Thomas Nelson, for extracts from: W. C. Dickinson and G. Donaldson (eds), *A Source Book of Scottish History* (1954). Hutchinson, for extracts from: Robert Ashton (ed.), *James I by his Contemporaries* (1969). Longman, for extracts from: S. J. Houston, *James I* (2nd edition, 1995); Roger Lockyer, *Buckingham. The Life and Political Career of George Villiers, First Duke of Buckingham 1592–1628* (1981) and *James VI and I* (1988); Michael A. R. Graves, *Elizabethan Parliaments 1559–1601* (2nd edition, 1996). Everyman, for extracts from: Lucy Hutchinson, *Memoirs of the Life of Colonel Hutchinson* (1995). Methuen, for extracts from: G. R. Elton, *England under the Tudors* (2nd edition, 1974). Clarendon Press, for extracts from: J. F. Larkin (ed.), *Stuart Royal Proclamations: Vol. 2. Royal Proclamations of King Charles I, 1625–46* (1983); S. R. Gardiner (ed.), *Constitutional Documents of the Puritan Revolution, 1625–1660* (3rd edition, 1906); Penry Williams, *The Later Tudors, England 1547–1603* (1998). The Provost and Fellows of Worcester College, Oxford/the Courtauld Institute, for Chapter 6, Source A. The Chatsworth Settlement Trustees/the Courtauld Institute, for Chapter 6, Source C. The Church of England Record Society, for extracts from Judith Maltby (ed.), 'Petitions for Episcopacy and the Book of Common Prayer on the Eve of the Civil War', in Stephen Taylor (ed.), *From Cranmer to Davidson: A Miscellany* (Church of England Record Society, 7, 1999).

1

JAMES VI AND THE ELIZABETHAN LEGACY

BACKGROUND NARRATIVE

Within a few hours of Elizabeth I's death at Richmond early on the morning of 24 March 1603, James VI of Scotland was proclaimed in London as James I of England. Three days later, a despatch rider, Sir Robert Carey, arrived in Edinburgh to convey the news to the King in person. James's accession to the English throne was remarkably peaceful: according to one contemporary there was 'no tumult, no contradiction, no disorder', and as he journeyed south into England his new subjects warmly welcomed him, 'their eyes flaming nothing but sparkles of affection'.[1] Early in May he arrived in London.

This opening chapter sets the scene for James's reign by considering two key issues. First, how far was the England that he inherited from Elizabeth a flawed inheritance that presented its new ruler with serious problems? Second, to what extent did his lengthy experience as King of Scotland prepare him for his new role and give him a training that could usefully be transferred to England? These two questions provide excellent starting-points for an account of English history under the early Stuarts.

ANALYSIS (1): TO WHAT EXTENT CAN THE ELIZABETHAN LEGACY BE CONSIDERED A *DAMNOSA HEREDITAS*, A PROBLEMATIC INHERITANCE?

Assessment of the nature of the Elizabethan legacy is of course central to any understanding of the reign of James and perhaps even his successors. On the one hand, if it is considered that the Queen bequeathed a governmental system that was in rude health, then it follows that the problems encountered by James were of his own making. For a long time this was the established picture, fashioned in the first instance by Elizabeth's own propaganda designed to extol the virtues of Gloriana, Virgin Queen and Protestant saviour, and latterly by Sir John Neale's classic biography published in 1934 in which he presented the image of an all-wise, all-competent national leader.[2] On the other hand, if it is reckoned that Elizabeth bequeathed a *damnosa hereditas*, then it follows that James was not the author of at least some of the problems he encountered.

A large body of writing favours this latter view, historians frequently concurring that there existed a 'crisis of the 1590s'.[3] Gordon Donaldson has concluded that 'the cares and burdens [of the Jacobean period] were not of James's making; they constituted the *damnosa hereditas* left by Elizabeth Tudor, a sovereign utterly careless of the well-being of her kingdom after her own demise, who had allowed problems to build up in her later years and whose reign had ended in anti-climax, in decline, almost in failure'.[4] More recently, J. A. Sharpe has argued that 'early in [James's] reign at least many of his problems arose from having to clear up the mess which his predecessor had left him'.[5] Certainly, in a number of respects Elizabeth seems to have left an awkward inheritance for her successor.

First, the country which James regarded as 'the land of promise' had in fact, by the time of his accession, been racked by the impact of eighteen years of war against Spain. In the county of Kent 6,000 men were impressed between 1591 and 1602 at a time when that county's total population was no more than 130,000. Since 1585 the total number of men impressed for service in the Netherlands, France, Portugal and Ireland was 105,810. To the detriment of trade, the pressure of war had demanded that the Queen commandeer ships for naval service. Local taxation escalated since counties were responsible for such things as the provision of stocks of arms and armour, the repair of coastal forts and the payment of muster masters. During the 1590s the levies of men and equipment for overseas service were costing each county up to £2,000 every year, added to which were the demands of prerogative taxation.

A forced loan was demanded in each of the years 1588, 1590, 1597 and 1601. Ship Money, a tax levied for the provision of ships, which was traditionally only paid by those communities on the coast, was now extended to inland areas.

Coupled with periodic outbreaks of plague and disastrous harvests in every year from 1594 to 1597, the pressures of war seem to have induced a malfunctioning of the relationship between the centre and the localities. By the time of the Queen's death wide-scale passive resistance to the demands of the Privy Council was commonplace. The county of Suffolk, for example, failed to respond to the Council's request for money in order to equip cavalry destined for Ireland. In March 1592 thirteen counties were identified as having failed to return certificates of their forces despite the fact that the Privy Council had requested them eighteen months earlier. The strongest opposition came to the demands for the payment of Ship Money. The Justices of the Peace of Suffolk, having put up persistent opposition to Ship Money, were accused by the Privy Council of having encouraged 'the people to discontentments [rather] than to concur in Her Majesty's service'.[6] In 1598 resistance was reported from Oxfordshire, Norfolk, Suffolk, Rutland, London and Coventry. London forced the Queen to drop her demand for ten ships in December 1596. Meanwhile, the overseas levies, composed mostly of 'either [the] old, diseased, boys or common rogues', mutinied rather than follow instructions.[7] In July 1602 a soldier stabbed his officer. Unsurprisingly, therefore, some historians have talked of James having inherited a 'slide to disaster' in the counties, country gentlemen having become dangerously alienated from the Court.[8]

Second, although the traditional historical verdict is that the Queen distributed patronage in a way which ensured that no group felt excluded from any hope of obtaining favour, she nevertheless bequeathed to James a dangerous factional imbalance. Always short of money, especially after 1585, Elizabeth lacked the means to lubricate the patronage system effectively. Thus, after 1598 Robert Cecil so dominated the administration that he deprived his rivals of access to the person of the monarch, a circumstance which drove Robert Devereux, Earl of Essex to rebellion in 1601. Consequently, 'James VI succeeded to a realm in which the control, no less than the fruits of patronage, were in the hands of one faction'.[9] From this state of affairs there might easily have sprung another rebellion if James had not very quickly met the desire for Court office among the nobility and gentry, pent up throughout Elizabeth's reign. He therefore repaid some of his political debts by doubling the size of the Privy Council (to twenty-six) and tripled the number of knights (to about 1,500) in the first year of his reign as James I.

Third, Elizabethan parsimony not only distorted the patronage system but ensured that by 1603 corruption in government circles was endemic. Consequently, the reputation of the Court was besmirched by a number of scandals involving the buying and selling of office and the milking of the royal coffers. For instance, George Goring, Receiver-General of the Court of Wards from 1584 to 1594, died owing the Crown £19,777 although his official salary was £66 per annum. Burghley's income as Master of the Wards for the two-year period 1596–1598 was £3,301, representing almost entirely receipts from private suitors as 'arrangement fees' for eleven grants of wardship at a time when his official salary was £133 per annum. Finally, Sir Thomas Shirley, Treasurer at War, enjoyed an income which ranged between £3,000 and £16,000 per annum, though his official salary was £365. As John Guy has concluded, 'the theory that there was a deterioration of public morality in the 1590s and 1600s [therefore] bears examination'.[10] It seemed that it was very much the case that 'for a [monarch] not to be bountiful were a fault'.[11]

Fourth, James inherited a Church which had been systematically plundered by Elizabeth and her predecessors. In 1590 Matthew Sutcliffe lamented how laymen had 'devoured the late lands and abbeys'.[12] Thus, recognising that many of the abuses in the Church, especially pluralism and non-residence, were the consequences of poverty, James sought to re-endow the Church, especially by liberating tithes from laymen and the universities. However, attempts to restore impropriated tithes to ministers were dashed on the rocks of vested economic interests among the laity and contributed to ill-feeling between James and the political nation.

Fifth, the last two Parliaments of Elizabeth (in 1597–1598 and 1601) proved to be the most fractious of the whole reign. Keenly fought disputes centred upon monopolies, responsible – among other things – for doubling the price of steel, tripling the price of starch and causing the price of imported salt to rise elevenfold. One MP complained of 'a country that groans under the burden' of monopolies and went on to call their owners 'bloodsuckers of the commonwealth'.[13] After a mob petitioned Parliament to complain that they were being 'imprisoned and robbed by monopolists' Robert Cecil cautioned against the 'people' being involved in public matters. The crisis was at last defused by the Queen agreeing that some monopolies 'should be presently repealed, some suspended, and none put in execution but such as should first have a trial according to the law for the good of her people'.[14] It seemed that James could realistically expect difficulties in his dealings with Parliament.

Sixth, the Queen's successors suffered especially from her decision to put political goodwill before fiscal efficiency. In particular, the Elizabethan regime failed to revise subsidy assessments in response to the extraordinary price inflation of the sixteenth century. Consequently, few taxpayers were assessed at anywhere near their actual wealth. One Sussex JP estimated that 'the rich were often rated . . . much too low, at not a fortieth part of their wealth'.[15] In a comment in Parliament in 1601, Raleigh suggested that 'our estates that be £30 or £40 in the Queen's books are not the hundredth part of our wealth'.[16] In 1601 the Earl of Derby was taxed on £400, though his rent roll was valued at £4,035 per annum. Inflation and static tax assessments, a reluctance to tax wage-earners alongside substantial property owners and a system which encouraged evasion thus combined to ensure a dramatic collapse in the yield of a subsidy, from £130,000 in the middle of Elizabeth's reign to £70,000 by 1621 and to £55,000 by 1628.

The Queen coped with the declining value of a subsidy by pursuing the dual policy of penny-pinching and selling royal lands – between 1589 and 1601 this last measure realised £608,505. However, the sale of Crown lands, combined with the fall in the value of money, resulted in a rapid decline in royal income from the Crown estates: from £200,000 in the 1530s, to £72,000 in 1619 and no more than £10,000 in the 1630s. Robert Cecil duly informed a friend in 1602 that 'all the [Crown] receipts are so short of issue, as my hairs stand upright to think of it'.[17] Moreover, Elizabeth bequeathed to her successor a debt totalling £365,254.

Faced with a political nation which seemed unable to acknowledge the devastating effect of inflation upon the value of a subsidy and, further-more, one which remained wedded and glued to the notion that during peacetime the Crown should 'live of its own', James was compelled to raise even greater amounts of revenue by those very prerogative means which MPs most resented – in particular, wardships, purveyance, impositions and the granting of monopolies. It was a dangerous vicious circle to which Elizabeth had given momentum.

Finally, the political nature of the Jacobean inheritance amounted to what John Morrill has called a 'dynastic conglomerate', an amalgamation of territories each with its own identity.[18] The only union that took place in 1603 was a union of the Crowns. Institutional separateness remained and induced a profound political instability that was present for the whole of the first half of the seventeenth century. England, Scotland and Ireland retained their own Parliaments, each of which was structurally different from the other two. The new King's government was made yet more difficult by the existence of three different Councils and legal systems and the fact that a significant minority of the inhabitants of the British Isles could not speak English, or any variant of it. Moreover, territories such as the Highlands and that part of Ireland outside of the Pale traditionally operated according to local allegiances and loyalties rather than any dictum from a distant government. Above all, in 1600 perhaps as many as one-third of the inhabitants of the British Isles were non-Protestant, the vast majority of the Irish population, large parts of Wales and the Highlands of Scotland adhering to Catholicism. In Scotland the national Church, although Protestant, differed in form from the Church of England.

Yet this negative picture of the Elizabethan legacy has been by no means fully accepted. In part this is because of a recognition that governmental structures continued to exist and government continued to function. There remained a considerable loyalty to the Court and Crown and general agreement about the need to implement laws. As John Guy has noted, 'in the 1590s tension between "Court" and "Country" was neither as ideological as was the opposition to Charles I, nor in most cases were deputy lieutenants and JPs expressing more than war-weariness and dislike of fiscal burdens'.[19] In this sense James did not inherit a 'slide to disaster'. Indeed, having demonstrated that 'the homogeneity of Court and Privy Council under Elizabeth was a major source of stability', Guy concludes that '"a slide to disaster" was inconceivable in the sixteenth century'.[20]

Historians have also pointed out that the Elizabethan Church settlement of 1559 – the famous *via media*, a middle way designed to allow the conscience of all but the most extreme Protestants to worship within the national Church – far from breaking down by 1603, was showing signs of having established healthy roots. It is no longer possible to argue that by failing to appease her Puritan critics by refusing to continue to reform the Church in a Protestant direction the Queen created impossible difficulties for her successors. By 1603 the greater part of the Puritans offered little threat to the stability of the state, and moreover had suffered a rebuttal of their criticisms when Richard Hooker offered a vigorous intellectual justification for the Church of England in his *Laws of Ecclesiastical Polity* published in the 1590s. However, the government also had to deal with the more extreme of the Puritans, known as Presbyterians: men like Thomas Cartwright, John Field, Walter Travers and Thomas Wilcox who rejected the Prayer Book as having been 'culled and picked out of that popish dunghill, the . . . mass book'.[21] Although, after failing to secure statutory redress of their grievances in the Parliaments of 1584 and 1586–1587, the Presbyterians suffered a loss of direction. Then, upon the defeat of the Armada in 1588, John Whitgift, the Archbishop of Canterbury (1583–1604), was able to turn his attention to the suppression of this element. In 1589 and 1590 the papers of leading members of the movement were seized and used to help prosecute nine Presbyterian ministers, including Thomas Cartwright. His colleague John Field had died in 1588.

There is therefore no evidence that the Presbyterian movement grew in strength as Elizabeth grew older – indeed the very opposite occurred. Nevertheless, there is no doubt that the practices and demands of even the more moderate Puritans created dissension. Bishop Fletcher of London described the effects of Puritan preachers in Essex as having provoked 'great quarrels and contentions, both in their civil bodies and among their ministers, the people divided and the priests taking part on both sides and at war with themselves, as well in matter of popular quarrels as points of doctrine'.[22] Indeed, disputes over the issue of predestination – the belief that God from the beginning had destined some men for eternal salvation and others for eternal damnation – were so bitter that they posed a very real threat to the stability of the regime. Though the Queen stifled the debate by forbidding any further discussion on the grounds that predestination was 'a matter tender and dangerous to weak, ignorant minds', these disputes signalled the possibility of a serious theological split at some point in the future.

Although Catholics were denied toleration, and periodically suffered severe persecution, their numbers nevertheless seem to have increased significantly. For example, the diocesan visitation of Lancashire in 1598 discovered 498 recusants, a number which had swelled to more than 3,500 by 1604. Figures for the North Riding of Yorkshire also show an increase in recusancy during this period.[23] Some historians have argued that this growth in the number of Catholics during Elizabeth's reign came to represent a threat to Protestant English liberties by 1603, and even that the origins of the Gunpowder Plot of 1605 can be traced back to this period. Yet it needs to be stressed that the Catholics remained loyal during the Armada campaign and the subsequent invasion scares. Moreover, the total Catholic community in 1603 was probably no more than 40,000 strong.

Finally, Sir John Neale's argument that the Elizabethan Commons was an institution growing in authority and political maturity, increasingly locked in political conflict over matters of state between Elizabeth and members of the Commons spearheaded by a vociferous 'Puritan choir', has been effectively challenged.[24] Historians such as Elton and Graves have demonstrated not only that Neale exaggerated levels of political conflict, but that he had failed to appreciate that many of the occasions on which the Commons apparently opposed the Crown were the consequences of divisions of opinion within the Court and Privy Council that extended into the Houses of Parliament.[25] Graves concluded that throughout the Tudor period Parliament 'continued to be a communion of crown and governing elite, acting as partners in the management of the kingdom . . . It served the interests of both the monarchy and the wider community of the realm.'[26]

Therefore, it is unsatisfactory to apply simple assessments of either 'good' or 'bad' to the Elizabethan legacy. While the Queen was at times to some degree cavalier with respect to her royal responsibilities, on other occasions, she lived up to her epithet Good Queen Bess. There is no denying that Elizabeth's last years were marked by the cumulative strain of a long war, even that Elizabethan fiscal inefficiencies facilitated the functional breakdown of the late 1620s. Yet she nevertheless provided her successor with, among other things, a regime in which a Protestant consensus had emerged and in which communications between the centre and the periphery continued to function. A study of the Elizabethan legacy does not reveal a high road to civil war.

Questions

1. In what ways, and to what extent, is it possible to talk of there having been 'a crisis of the 1590s'?
2. How far would you agree with the notion that Elizabeth bequeathed her successor a state that was in the best of health?

ANALYSIS (2): TO WHAT EXTENT DID JAMES VI'S EXPERIENCES AS KING OF SCOTLAND PREPARE HIM FOR GOVERNMENT OF ENGLAND?

It is important to understand James's experiences and achievements as King of Scotland in their own terms and not to see them simply as a prelude to his rule of England. His government of Scotland needs to be set in the context of Scottish kingship, and not judged by English criteria or expectations. The constitutional and religious traditions of the two nations were significantly different, as were their economies and social structures. James was, in Jenny Brown's words, 'the last and greatest exponent of the old style of Scottish kingship',[27] and when he reflected on his rule of Scotland, in *The True Law of Free Monarchies* (1598) and the *Basilikon Doron* (1599), he was writing for Scottish rather than English readers.

That said, it seems that from the early 1580s onwards, James realised that he was Elizabeth I's likeliest eventual successor, and his conduct as King of Scotland was at least partly shaped by a wish to avoid doing anything that might jeopardise his chances of inheriting the English throne. He was in touch with Elizabeth's Secretary of State, Robert Cecil, from at least the spring of 1601 (if not earlier), and when the old Queen died in March 1603 an efficient plan ensured James's remarkably smooth accession. James so clearly coveted the English Crown that it is surely appropriate to ask how well prepared he was for his new task, and to assess which aspects of his experiences as King of Scotland were readily adaptable to English conditions. In early modern Scotland, as in England, political stability depended very largely on the relationship between the monarch and the most powerful subjects, the nobility and the lairds. James grew up in a period when the Crown's authority had been seriously weakened first by his mother Mary Queen of Scots' disastrous rule, and then by his own minority. Yet, by a combination of determination and pragmatic common sense, James had succeeded by 1603 in regaining control and indeed raising royal authority to a stronger position than for decades. The difficulty of this task was made very plain to James in August 1582, when the Earl of Gowrie and a group of other nobles hostile to James's favourite, Esme Stewart, Duke of Lennox, seized James at Ruthven Castle and refused to release him until he ordered Lennox to leave Scotland. James was held for nearly a year and had no option but to capitulate, although he was able to secure Gowrie's execution as a traitor two years later.

Thereafter, James treated the Scottish nobles with great patience, and always preferred to handle dissidents, such as the Earls of Bothwell and Huntly, by persuasion rather than coercion. He shrewdly realised that it was better to exploit the inherent factionalism of the Scottish nobility, and to pursue a policy of divide and rule, rather than adopt a more heavy-handed approach that risked uniting the nobles against him. James deliberately kept out of bitter feuds such as those between the Earls of Moray and Huntly in the north-east, or between the Campbells and the MacDonalds in the western Highlands, and thus avoided becoming identified too closely with one particular faction. Although this approach could not ensure complete stability, the general climate did become more respectful towards royal authority, and the Gowrie Conspiracy (an attempt to kidnap James in August 1600 that remains somewhat mysterious) exemplified a kind of behaviour that had become much less common by the end of the sixteenth century. James carefully associated the Crown with the rule of law and in so doing inculcated greater respect for both; in the *Basilikon Doron* he advised his son to 'teach your nobility to keep your laws as precisely as the meanest [subjects]'.[28] James also stressed the vital importance of respecting the nobility and of being personally accessible to them, so that none should feel marginalised (see Source E). This was no less relevant to the handling of the English nobility and gentry, and James's patient, pragmatic and open approach stood him in excellent stead when he moved to his new southern kingdom.

While recognising the importance of informal contacts with the political elite, James also had to interact with them through formal institutions, most notably the Scottish Parliament. This body stood in marked contrast to the English Parliament. It consisted of a single chamber (rather than separate Houses of Lords and Commons), in which were represented nobles, lairds, burgesses, bishops and officers of state. Through the committee known as the Lords of the Articles, the monarch was able to control membership of the Parliament as well as what business was discussed, and James made highly effective use of these powers. In that sense the Scottish Parliament was much easier to control than the English one. Whereas it was relatively easy for James to ensure the passage of legislation, the decentralised nature of Scottish government made it much more difficult to enforce on the ground (the ecclesiastical reforms contained in the Five Articles of Perth, passed by the Scottish Parliament in 1621, are a good example of this). In England the situation was the reverse: English Parliaments had a strong sense of their own rights and privileges and were extremely sensitive to the slightest hint of royal encroachment. Monarchs needed to manage the two Houses very carefully in order to secure the passage of acts (statutes), but once on the statute book England's centralised legal and administrative structures then ensured that they could be put into operation without much difficulty. It inevitably took James time to adjust to this difference, which may well explain why he became so demoralised in the face of parliamentary opposition to his proposals for a union of the kingdoms in 1604–1608: as John Morrill has suggested, James was 'quickly discouraged at falling at what in Scotland would have been the lowest hurdle'.[29] His experience of the Scottish Parliament helps to explain a great deal about James's problematic relations with its English counterpart.

There were other important differences as well. By the 1530s, the supremacy and omnicompetence of statute as the highest form of human law in England gave Parliament a legislative monopoly that never existed in Scotland, where Parliament's consent was not necessary for laws to be valid. It was equally possible for laws to be assented to by Conventions of the three Estates (nobles, leaders of the Kirk and burgesses) or just of the nobility: between 1588 and 1603, for example, there were forty-nine such Conventions but only five Parliaments.[30] It was possible in Scotland, in a way that it never was in England, for the monarch to introduce laws or taxes without Parliament's consent. James was only describing accepted Scottish practice when he wrote in the *Basilikon Doron* that: 'albeit the King make daily statutes and ordinances . . . without any advice of Parliament or Estates; yet it lies in the power of no Parliament, to make any kind of law or statute, without his sceptre be to it, for giving it the force of a law'.[31] The situation that awaited him in England was utterly different, for there Parliament jealously guarded its right to assent to laws and taxes, and the monarch was far weaker acting alone than when collaborating with Parliament.

Scottish practices for making laws in turn shaped James's view of the rule of law. Scotland's legal system was – and remains – very different from England's: in particular, it was far more influenced by the Roman and civil law codes that were very widespread on the continent. There was no equivalent to the English common law, and as a result common law principles such as trial by jury or innocence until proven guilty never really took hold in Scotland. Roman and civil law invested greater powers in the magistrate than was the case in England, and this carried over into a more authoritarian view of the relationship between the monarch and the rule of law. Although some Scottish theorists, including James's old tutor George Buchanan, argued for a contractual idea of monarchy, James successfully asserted that 'the King is above the law', even though he conceded that 'a good king will frame all his actions to be according to the law', without being obliged to.[32] This stood in marked contrast to the English constitutional tradition summed up by the thirteenth-century legalist Henry de Bracton in the axiom that 'the monarch must be under the law'.[33] This meant that James would have to tread warily in his new kingdom, for the English elite was highly sensitive to any hint that the monarch saw himself as above the law.

In some ways, an area of comparable touchiness in Scotland was the Kirk. Whereas in England the monarch's supremacy over the Church was accepted, but his relationship with the law remained sensitive, in Scotland the situation was the reverse. Throughout his reign, James was dogged by the thorny issue of how far his royal authority extended to the Kirk. During the reign of his Catholic mother, the Scottish Reformed Kirk had developed a structure in which it was governed by a General Assembly, independently of the monarch. This ultimately led some Presbyterians, most notably Andrew Melville, to argue that Church and state formed 'two kingdoms' which were mutually exclusive: this claim was most clearly stated in the *Second Book of Discipline* (1578), which also condemned the office of bishop. However, other Scottish Protestants, such as Patrick Adamson, Archbishop of St Andrews, defended bishops and were more sympathetic towards royal influence over the Church. With their assistance, James secured the passage in May 1584 of the 'Black Acts' which reaffirmed episcopal government and asserted that supremacy over the Church should rest with the Crown-in-Parliament. But many Presbyterians remained deeply unhappy with this, and in 1592 the 'Golden Act' authorised the Presbyterian system of courts and deprived the bishops of authority. Yet in the years that followed the Presbyterian system failed to establish itself throughout Scotland, and by 1600 James had secured the appointment of titular bishops who held the title of bishop and sat in Parliament but lacked ecclesiastical jurisdiction or status.

James thus found himself caught between two potentially hostile groups: a resilient Catholic community located particularly in certain areas of the north-east, the western Highlands and the Western Isles; and the Presbyterians, concentrated especially in the Lowlands, who resented royal interference in the Church. Melville summed up the Presbyterian outlook in 1596 when he called James 'God's silly [i.e. weak] vassal', and told him that 'there are two kings and two kingdoms in Scotland. There is Jesus Christ the king and his kingdom whose subject King James VI is, and of whose kingdom not a king, nor a lord, nor a head, but a member.'[34] James handled this problem very deftly by trying to steer a middle course that would win over as many moderates as possible. He remained patient, avoided aggression as much as he could, and adopted a gradualist strategy by which episcopacy was nurtured in the Church little by little. All of this turned out to be an excellent preparation for his later role as Supreme Governor of the Church of England. The episcopalian structure of the English Church represented the broad direction in which he hoped to see the Scottish Kirk move, and in 1610 his patience bore fruit when three Scottish bishops were consecrated by English bishops at Westminster, thereby restoring the normal episcopal succession in Scotland. Above all, the ability to strike a balance, to win over moderates and avoid extremes, was no less crucial to the stability of the English Church than it was in Scotland.

James's experiences as King of Scotland were thus a mixed blessing. In some ways – most notably his pragmatic approach to the political elite and to the Church – James's skills could be readily applied, with some adaptation, to the English scene. On the other hand, there were some major institutional contrasts between the two kingdoms, especially in their Parliaments and their legal systems, that would require careful learning and adjustment. When James left Scotland in 1603 he promised to return annually. He only went back once, in 1617, when what he called his 'salmon-like instinct' prompted a visit intended especially to promote the Five Articles of Perth.[35] These were one of a number of means by which James sought to foster greater congruity between the institutions of his three kingdoms. By then he had learnt, from direct experience, how much they differed one from another. As he soon realised in the years after 1603, experience of ruling one kingdom could never be more than a very partial and incomplete preparation for ruling another.

Questions

1. What were James VI's principal aims as King of Scotland, and how successful was he in achieving them by 1603?
2. 'I am ever for the medium in every thing' (James VI and I).[36] How far did James's rule over Scotland up to 1603 bear this out?

SOURCES

1. PROBLEMS IN PARLIAMENT, 1601

Source A: From a speech on monopolies to Parliament, 20 November 1601.

Mr Martin said: I speak for a town that grieves and pines and for a country that groaneth under the burden of monstrous and unconscionable . . . monopolies of starch, tin, fish, cloth, oil, vinegar, salt and I know not what: nay, what not? The principal commodities both of my town and country are ingrossed [i.e. taken completely] into the hands of these bloodsuckers of the commonwealth.

Source B: The Speaker delivers a message from the Queen to Parliament, 25 November 1601.

It pleased her majesty to command me to attend upon her yesterday . . . from whom I am to deliver unto you all her majesty's most gracious message . . . She said, that partly by intimation of her council and partly by divers petitions that have been delivered unto her, both [when] going to chapel and walking abroad, she understood that divers patents [i.e. a form of monopoly] that she had granted were grievous unto her subjects . . . But, she said, she never assented to grant anything that was evil in itself and [if that were so] she herself would take present order for reformation thereof.

Source C: From a speech by Robert Cecil, the chief minister to the Queen, to the Parliament of 1601, 25 November 1601.

We are not secret amongst ourselves ... why, Parliament matters are ordinarily talked of in the streets. I have heard myself, being in my coach, these words spoken aloud: 'God prosper those that further the overthrow of these monopolies! God send [that] the prerogative touch not our liberty ... ' The time was never more apt to disorder, or [to] make ill interpretations of good meanings. I think these persons would be glad that all sovereignty were converted into popularity.

Source D: The Queen addresses a deputation from the Commons, 30 November 1601.

Though God hath raised me high, yet this I count the glory of my crown, that I have reigned with your loves ... I was never so much enticed with the glorious name ... or royal authority of a queen, as delighted that God hath made me his instrument to maintain his truth and glory and to defend his kingdom from peril, dishonour, tyranny and oppression ... Though you have had and may have many mightier and wiser princes sitting on this seat, yet you never had nor shall have any that will love you better.

Questions

1. Read Source A. Explain why monopolies produced so much resentment. [3]
*2. What can a historian deduce from Source B about the political methods of Elizabeth? [5]
3. Noting its language and content, as well as referring to your own knowledge, how reliable do you consider Source A for a historian researching into reasons for the hatred of monopolies? [4]
4. Compare the effectiveness of the speeches made by Cecil and Elizabeth, Sources C and D. [5]
5. 'The time was never more apt to disorder' (Source C). Referring to these documents and your own knowledge, how appropriate do you consider this remark about the 1590s? [8]

Worked answer

*2. *[Having identified relevant parts of the Source it is important to explain their meaning and comment upon what they imply.]*

In this Source we can see Elizabeth employing a number of devices in order to appease the political nation and defuse the crisis over monopolies. First, she advertises her accessibility by stating that not only has she listened to 'her council' but that she has been open to the reception of petitions while 'going to chapel and walking abroad'. Second, she makes it clear that she has understood her subjects' grievances and that 'she herself' will ensure the 'reformation thereof' – but only of 'anything that was evil in itself', a sufficiently vague phrase to allow her room for manoeuvre. Third, it is notable that the Queen is careful to distance herself from the effects of 'grievous' patents, insisting that 'she never assented to grant anything that was evil in itself'. Finally, by employing the Speaker to deliver her message rather than appear in person herself before Parliament, the Queen avoided becoming entangled in an unseemly debate about the nature of the royal prerogative. It is also clear that the Speaker is simply reporting what was said at his meeting with Elizabeth, bestowing upon the Queen the ability perhaps to argue at some later date that she had been misrepresented.

SOURCES

2. JAMES VI's ABILITIES AS KING OF SCOTLAND

Source E: From James's *Basilikon Doron* (1599).

Acquaint yourself [with all] ... your barons and gentlemen, and be in your giving access so open and affable to every rank of honest persons ... The more frequently that your Court can be garnished with them, think it the more your honour, acquainting and employing them in all your greatest affairs, since it is they [who] must be your arms and executors of your laws.

Source F: From a letter from Robert Bowes to Sir Francis Walsingham, 3 July 1583.

Having long desired to draw his nobility to unity and concord, and to be known to be a universal King, indifferent to them all, therefore his meaning was only to seek the accomplishment of these two points.

Source G: From an act passed by James VI and the Scottish Parliament in 1584.

Our sovereign lord and his three estates assembled in this present Parliament ratifies and approves and perpetually confirms the royal power and authority over all estates as well spiritual as temporal within this realm in the person of the King's majesty our sovereign lord, his heirs and successors.

Source H: From James's *Basilikon Doron* (1599).

Some fiery-spirited men in the ministry . . . began to fantasise to themselves a democratic form of government . . . Their conceited parity can neither stand with the order of the Church nor the peace of a Commonwealth and well ruled monarchy . . . Cherish no man more than a good pastor, hate no man more than a proud Puritan.

Source I: From Sir Henry Wotton's first-hand account of James VI, written for the Grand Duke of Tuscany in about June 1602.

In the handling of affairs of state he . . . does not settle even the smallest matters without counsel . . . From his frequent creations of Marquises, Earls and Barons, one may surmise that he is not greatly subject to jealousy of the magnates; although some may be of the opinion that this is done more frequently there [i.e. in Scotland] than in . . . England, because the King seeks to oblige his subjects with honours and titles, not having any other way of gratifying them . . . He used to be more under the control of the ministers of religion than he is now . . . He does not now keep an ordinary guard about his person, either disliking the expense, or resting himself upon the love of his people, which he is accustomed to call the true guard of princes.

Questions

*1. (i) Read Source F. Comment on the phrase 'a universal King, indifferent to them all'. [2]

(ii) Read Source H. What do you think James meant by 'a democratic form of government'? [2]

2. What can the historian learn from Sources E and F about James's handling of the Scottish nobility? [4]

3. What was the purpose of Source G, and how successful was it in achieving it? [4]

4. How far does Source I indicate the success of the policies that James advocated in Sources E–H? [6]

5. Using these sources and your own knowledge, compare and contrast James's approaches to the Scottish nobility and the Scottish Kirk. [7]

Worked answer

*1. *[These questions carry only a small number of marks so answers should be quite brief. Focus closely on the meanings of these phrases and what they reveal about James's aims and motives.]*

(i) James's wish to be 'a universal King' means that he wanted to be – and be seen to be – the King of all his noble subjects, and to avoid becoming associated with just one particular faction or group. He wanted to treat them all fairly, and the word 'indifferent' here means impartial and without any favourites among them.

(ii) By 'democratic', James means an equal form of government, without the hierarchy of bishops, deans and other senior clergy. He disliked the claims of the more committed Presbyterians, and felt that in general a hierarchical structure of church offices, including episcopacy, suited the Crown's interests better than the 'parity' of ministers advocated by the likes of Andrew Melville.

2

JAMES I

Religion and the Church

BACKGROUND NARRATIVE

The Church of England which James inherited from Elizabeth was in a state of uneasy equilibrium. The Elizabethan Settlement had consciously attempted to 'comprehend' a wide range of different religious outlooks within a broad Church; yet, in so doing, it had frustrated the hopes of many, and the significant numbers who had despaired of ever winning the old Queen's support for their proposals turned enthusiastically to James, hoping that he would introduce the reforms they desired. The 'Puritans', those who sought 'further reformation' of the Church and wished to cleanse it of echoes of Catholicism (such as vestments, bishops and the Prayer Book), presented their demands to James in the so-called Millenary Petition (April 1603). The King subsequently discussed these demands, and made some concessions to them, at the Hampton Court Conference (14–18 January 1604). At the other end of the religious spectrum, English Catholics regretted that James did not introduce as much toleration as they had hoped, but despaired of doing anything about it, apart from a minority of extremists who attempted to blow up the King and both Houses of Parliament in the Gunpowder Plot of November 1605. This generated an anti-popish furore that led to the passing of two penal laws against English Catholics in January 1606, one of which obliged them to take an Oath of Allegiance to the King.[1]

Elizabeth's long-serving Archbishop of Canterbury, John Whitgift, died in February 1604, and James appointed the equally anti-Puritan Richard Bancroft to succeed him. Yet James consistently sought to moderate Bancroft's more stringent actions against the Puritans, and chose as his successor the moderate George Abbot, who was Archbishop of Canterbury from March 1611 until his death in August 1633.

After the turbulence of the years 1603–1606, James largely succeeded in defusing overt religious controversy within England during the central part of his reign. In this period he also introduced a number of reforms intended to bring the Churches of Ireland and Scotland into a closer affinity with the Church of England. The most notable of these reforms were the Irish Articles of 1615, which were closely modelled on the Calvinist Lambeth Articles of 1595, and the Five Articles of Perth (accepted by the General Assembly of the Scottish Kirk in 1618, and by the Scottish Parliament in 1621), which tried to discourage Scots from regarding English practices such as observing Holy Days or kneeling at communion as idolatrous.

James consistently maintained his Protestant credentials, for example by sending representatives to the Synod of Dort in 1619 which condemned the anti-Calvinist writings of Jacobus Arminius. Yet in his final years, the King came under growing criticism for allegedly being too sympathetic towards Catholicism. The European context was vital in explaining why this happened. From the summer of 1618 onwards the continent gradually became embroiled in the Thirty Years' War, a bitter and protracted conflict between the forces of Catholicism and Protestantism that eventually engulfed large parts of central and western Europe. The Catholic powers enjoyed considerable military successes, especially early on, yet, to the horror of many of his more strongly Protestant subjects, James persisted in his dream of marrying his son Charles to a Catholic princess (the 'Spanish match'). Such a marriage alliance formed a central part of James's cherished ideal of reuniting the Protestant and Catholic powers of Europe. Some members of his last Parliament (February–May 1624) were also alarmed at his apparent leniency towards those clerics – such as Richard Montagu – who sought to minimise the doctrinal and institutional differences between the Churches of England and Rome. Instead, in August 1622 James issued new Directions to Preachers which forbade public attacks on either Puritans or Catholics. But by the early 1620s, in a climate of international warfare, James's attempts to preserve peace and stability within the Church were becoming increasingly difficult to sustain, and his final years were clouded by growing religious tensions within England.

ANALYSIS (1): BY WHAT MEANS, AND TO WHAT EXTENT, DID JAMES CREATE AN EFFECTIVE MIDDLE WAY IN RELIGIOUS AFFAIRS?

In his opening speech to his first English Parliament, on 19 March 1604, James I declared: 'I could wish from my heart, that it would please God to make me one of the members of such a general Christian union in religion, as laying wilfulness aside on both hands, we might meet in the middest, which is the centre and perfection of all things.'[2] This statement neatly summed up James's ideal of religious unity, in which the creation of a middle way would allay extremes and enable moderates of all hues to co-exist peacefully within a broad national Church. The pursuit of unity was the guiding principle of James's religious policies throughout his reign, and precisely paralleled the 'reunion of Christendom' which this peacemaker King sought in his foreign policy.

James faced two principal threats to his promotion of religious unity: the Catholics and the Puritans. He handled both these dangers by adopting the same basic strategy, which was to win over as many moderates as possible and to exclude only those radicals who actively sought to overthrow the established Church, or who presented a political challenge to his authority as Supreme Governor of the Church. In both cases he was concerned more to secure the basic loyalty and co-operation of as many as possible than to enforce precise conformity, and it is worth examining his treatment of each group in turn.

James's first major decision as Supreme Governor of the Church was to summon a number of bishops and other clergy, including several Puritans, to a conference at Hampton Court in January 1604. This was in response to the Millenary Petition, and Kenneth Fincham and Peter Lake have described its purpose thus: 'The Hampton Court conference was primarily a premeditated attempt to settle the issue of Puritanism once and for all by driving a wedge between the moderate and radical wings of Puritan opinion. The moderates were to be fully and finally integrated into the national church, while the extremists were to be expelled or repressed.'[3] James made it absolutely clear that he classified those who wished to abolish bishops and establish a Presbyterian model along Scottish lines as subversive radicals, a view that he summed up in the maxim 'No Bishop, no King'.[4] But James carefully distanced himself from the advocates of strict conformity, such as Bishop Barlow of Lincoln, and instead showed himself ready to make a number of important concessions to moderate Puritan opinion. In particular he promised better endowments to improve the quality of the clergy and reduce pluralism and non-residence; a new translation of the Bible was commissioned, subsequently published as the Authorised Version (or 'King James Bible') of 1611; and new Canons were issued in September 1604 which accepted the existence of lecturers or preachers, and also permitted 'prophesyings', the Puritan discussions of biblical texts which Elizabeth I had prohibited from the 1570s onwards.

The price of these concessions was that clergy were required to accept the basic framework and institutional structures of the Church of England. Specifically, the 1604 Canons obliged them to sign a statement declaring their acceptance of the royal supremacy, the Prayer Book and the Thirty-Nine Articles, together with the clerical hierarchy of bishops, priests and deacons, and agreeing to wear surplices while conducting services. James saw these requirements as a way 'to discern the affections of persons, whether quiet or turbulent'.[5] Clergy were given until the end of November 1604 to comply, and only somewhere between 73 and 83 beneficed clergy (out of a total of around 9,000) were deprived for failing to do so.

Thereafter, James regarded signed acceptance of these basic tenets, rather than exact ceremonial conformity, as the crucial test. This approach helped to appease the 'godly', such as the Puritan gentry of Northamptonshire, who had petitioned James in February 1605 to proceed moderately against godly clergy who 'by their conscionable and sincere teaching . . . have proved lights of great comfort and furtherance to us and all others your Majesty's subjects'.[6] In practice, James pursued just such an approach, and during the entire period 1611–1625 only two ministers were deprived of their livings because they refused to conform. Much more typical was the experience of John Cotton, the godly minister of Boston, Lincolnshire, who objected to kneeling to receive communion, and did not ask his congregation to do so either. However, because he showed a willingness to discuss forms of worship with his bishop, John Williams, Cotton was not penalised for his failure to observe the finer points of ceremonial conformity. Thus, as Kenneth Fincham and Peter Lake have written, 'moderate Puritans who held misgivings about aspects of the rites and discipline of the Church were accommodated within it since they posed no threat to the stability of church or state'.[7]

A broadly similar approach characterised James's treatment of the English Catholic community. Here again, his pursuit of unity led him to make a distinction between moderates and extremists. He tended to play down the doctrinal differences between the Churches of England and Rome; instead, his main concern was with Catholic opposition to the royal supremacy, and especially with papal claims to depose foreign rulers. Those who presented a direct political threat, and believed that rebellion against the enemies of Rome offered a route to salvation, he denounced as 'factious stirrers of sedition and perturbers of the common wealth'.[8] By contrast, the Venetian Ambassador was informed early in James's reign that 'as long as the Catholics remain quiet and decently hidden they will neither be hunted nor persecuted', and James insisted that he would 'be a friend to their persons if they be good subjects'.[9] Not even the Gunpowder Plot deflected him from this overarching objective. The second of the two penal laws of January 1606 required Catholics to take an oath of allegiance, the purpose of which was, in James's words, 'to make a separation between so many of my subjects, who although they were otherwise popishly affected, yet retained in their hearts the print of their natural duty to their sovereign; and those who . . . thought diversity of religion a safe pretext for all kind of treasons and rebellions against their sovereign'.[10] In James's eyes, willingness to take the oath provided the key test of Catholic moderation, much as accepting the 1604 Canons did for Puritans. He believed that the recusancy laws should be implemented primarily against those Catholic 'traitors' who refused to take the oath; beyond that the laws were only enforced intermittently.[11] In the main, provided that they kept their heads down, Catholics could live quietly under James, and some – most notably the Earl of Northampton and other members of the Howard family – rose to major political prominence.

James's commitment to religious unity thus led him to try to make the Church of England as comprehensive as possible: he hoped that a plurality of opinion could be tolerated within a broad framework. The only people who were excluded were those who refused to accept a few basic tenets, above all the royal supremacy and the episcopalian structure of the Church, or who attempted to subvert Church and state. Furthermore, in his appointments of bishops James consciously promoted a wide range of opinions in order to give the Church as broad a base of support as possible. Although in 1604 James appointed the anti-Puritan Richard Bancroft to succeed John Whitgift as Archbishop of Canterbury, he was in turn succeeded in 1611 by a much more tolerant figure, George Abbot, who was a mainstream Calvinist. This diversity characterised the Jacobean bench of bishops as a whole. At one end could be found Puritan figures, strongly committed to a preaching ministry, such as the Archbishop of York, Toby Matthew, or the Bishop of London, John King. At the other, bishops such as Lancelot Andrewes at Winchester, or Richard Neile, successively at Rochester, Lichfield, Durham and York, staunchly upheld a ceremonial style of worship and opposed concessions to Puritan opinion. In between stood many moderate men, with a variety of different emphases, of whom Abbot was fairly typical.

James's willingness to promote bishops who represented a range of different outlooks served to enhance the quality not only of the episcopate but of the clergy more widely. During James's reign the general standard of the clergy, the overwhelming majority of whom had graduated from Oxford or Cambridge, was so high that Joseph Hall, later Bishop of Exeter and of Norwich, remarked in a sermon in 1624 that 'the clergy of Britain are the wonder of the world'.[12] James's relations with his bishops were consistently better than Elizabeth's had been, and no fewer than six of them were appointed to the Privy Council.

The diversity of clerical appointments reflected the King's more general conviction that no one point of view held a monopoly on the truth, and provided that they accepted the basic framework of the Church of England, complete with bishops, the Prayer Book and the royal supremacy, moderates of all persuasions were welcomed within it. Much of the effectiveness of the Jacobean 'middle way' in religious affairs thus rested on James's wish to make the Church as broad and inclusive as possible. But it was increasingly difficult to maintain such a peaceful middle way amid the international conflict that engulfed Europe in the years after 1618, and by the time James died religious opinion in England was becoming more polarised and enflamed than at any time during his reign.

Questions

1. How far did James succeed in achieving his goal of 'a general Christian union in religion'?
2. To what extent was James's treatment of Puritans and Catholics guided by a similar strategy?

ANALYSIS (2): HOW SUCCESSFUL WAS JACOBEAN RELIGIOUS POLICY?

J. P. Kenyon summed up much recent research on the Jacobean Church when he called James's reign 'a period of eirenic compromise' in English religious history, and suggested that 'James's finest achievement was the establishment of a religious détente which had entirely eluded Elizabeth.'[13] Against this, other historians have suggested that the Jacobean religious equilibrium was at best fragile, and that it disintegrated rapidly from about 1618 onwards. In assessing these different interpretations, much depends on which portion of the reign is examined, and a similarly mixed picture emerges when we consider the 'British' dimension of Jacobean religious policy.

During the opening years of James's reign, from 1603 to about 1606, he established the broad outlines of his religious policy and his basic approach towards Catholics and Puritans. His central aim was to make the Church of England as broad as possible, and to comprehend within it as wide a range of beliefs and practices as possible. He wished to steer a 'middle way' between Rome on the one hand and radical Protestantism on the other, and to foster a Church that embraced moderates of all persuasions; only extremists were to be excluded. For over a decade, from 1603 until about 1618–1620, James succeeded to a considerable extent in defusing religious tension within England. One of the most telling symptoms of this was the way in which the parliamentary sessions of 1606 to 1607, 1610 and 1614 saw much less vociferous religious debate than those before or after, and certainly than most Elizabethan Parliaments. That did not mean that everyone was happy with the existing state of the Jacobean Church: in July 1610, for example, the Commons presented a Petition on Religion to the King in which they requested the tougher enforcement of the laws against recusancy, permission for deprived ministers to be allowed to preach provided that they 'live quietly and peaceably in their callings, and shall not . . . impugn things established by public authority', and tougher measures against pluralism and non-residence.[14] James replied that he did not lump all offenders together and offered to try to distinguish between deprived ministers, 'in regard of better hope of conformity in some than in others, although they be in the same degree offenders by our laws'.[15] This flexible response helped to quieten down the agitation, and in general the Puritans perceived James as more sympathetic than his predecessor. Most of them felt that the Jacobean Church was moving in the right direction, albeit too slowly, and it was significant that in 1629 John Pym tried to include James in a list of 'Fathers of the Church'.[16]

Another indication of the success of Jacobean religious policy lay in the remarkably low numbers of people at either end of the religious spectrum who opted out of the Church. A few extreme Protestant sectarians, such as the Family of Love, boycotted the Church entirely and formed separatist congregations or conventicles. Some others departed to make a new life in the Netherlands or the American colonies;

the latter included the Pilgrim Fathers. But these complete separatists remained small in number during James's reign. Far more common were the 'semi-separatists': those prepared to attend the official church services as long as they could supplement them with extra sermons, prayer meetings, Bible-study groups and other 'godly' practices. As shown, for example, by the official acceptance of 'prophesyings' provided they were licensed by a bishop, these voluntary religious activities of the 'hotter sort of Protestants' were in some ways less constrained than they had been under Elizabeth.

Similarly, many Catholics were 'church-papists', who attended church services as well as worshipping secretly as Catholics, rather than 'recusants', who boycotted church services entirely. One of the penal laws of January 1606 introduced an annual fine of £20 for recusants. Although this brought as much as £8,000 a year into the Exchequer by 1614, in practice it was only levied patchily and sporadically. The period of greatest leniency towards Catholics was between about 1613 and 1621. There was also a link between the treatment of Catholics at home and developments in foreign policy. The twelve-year truce between the Dutch Republic and Spain in 1609–1621 helped to calm Protestant fears of Catholic aggrandisement. However, this international climate was to change dramatically during the final years of James's reign.

All these indications of the success of Jacobean religious policy need to be balanced against other less favourable evidence. In some ways James's management of the Church amounted to a sustained exercise in damage limitation, an attempt to contain a range of opinions within the Church by requiring subscription to a minimum of tenets. Yet the under-lying problem of religious diversity was not solved, or even addressed. James tried not to enflame religious tempers, but in so doing it could be argued that he glossed over divisions rather than resolved them.

These points can also be applied to the 'British' dimension of James's religious policies. James's desire to be 'King of Great Britain', the title that he adopted by royal proclamation in October 1604, was reflected in his attempts to bring the Churches of England, Scotland and Ireland into closer 'congruity' with each other.[17] He was not, however, seeking to make them uniform with each other, and the three kingdoms remained fundamentally different in their religious character. The Irish Articles of 1615 were closely modelled on the Calvinist Lambeth Articles of 1595, but the Church of Ireland represented an embattled minority within a population that remained overwhelmingly Catholic. In practice, Irish recusancy laws were a dead letter. In Scotland, James developed an episcopate and introduced a Court of High Commission modelled on that in England. Despite considerable opposition, he secured the acceptance of the Five Articles of Perth, the most contentious of which required the observation of saints' days and kneeling at communion. Many Scottish Presbyterians found such practices deeply offensive, and although the Five Articles were on the statute book from 1621, it was not always easy to enforce them. The vast majority of Protestant Scots continued to regard their Kirk as more purely and completely reformed than the Church of England, and James's strategy of drawing the two closer together enjoyed at best a limited and gradual success.

But perhaps the most serious setbacks to James's religious policies occurred in the final years of his reign when the outbreak of continental warfare between Protestants and Catholics greatly increased religious anxieties and rendered it much more difficult to sustain the ideals of unity and a middle way. In particular, Catholic military successes made English Puritans extremely sensitive to any apparent sign of the covert infiltration of popery. They resented the King's Declaration of Sports (May 1618) which, by licensing various recreations on a Sunday, appeared to threaten the Puritan ideal of the Sabbath. There was also widespread hostility towards James's attempts to secure a 'Spanish match' for the Prince of Wales, and considerable rejoicing when this scheme collapsed in the autumn of 1623.

Above all, many feared the promotion within the Church of anti-Calvinist clerics who advocated a 'ceremonialist' style of worship and regarded the Church of England as closer to Rome than to the reformed Churches of Scotland or the continent. Such divines, often branded 'Arminians' because their theology was thought to resemble that of Jacobus Arminius, included figures like William Laud and Richard Neile. James was as concerned as ever to calm religious tempers, and his Directions to Preachers in August 1622 condemned public attacks on both Puritans and papists. Yet in the early 1620s it was the more militant Puritans who, driven by fears of popery, presented the most vociferous threat to religious harmony. In 1624 there was a bitter outcry when Richard Montagu published a pamphlet entitled *A New Gag for an Old Goose* in which he condemned predestination and played down the doctrinal differences between the Churches of England and Rome. Some members of the Commons denounced Montagu as a papist and demanded his impeachment, but when James retorted that 'if this is to be a papist, so am I a papist', the Commons backed off and referred the matter to Archbishop Abbot.[18] However, James was not necessarily any more in favour of anti-Calvinists than hitherto. When, in 1621, Buckingham strongly pushed for Laud's appointment as Bishop of St David's, James replied: 'The plain truth is, that I keep Laud back from all place of rule and authority, because I find he hath a restless spirit, and cannot see when matters are well, but loves to toss and change, and to bring things to a pitch of reformation floating in his own brain, which may endanger the steadfastness of that which is in good pass.' He only agreed to Laud's appointment with the greatest reluctance and warned Buckingham: 'Then take him to you, but on my soul you will repent it.'[19] These were truly prophetic remarks, the shrewdness of which was to become all too evident in the years after James's death. For Laud's attempts to impose conformity and uniformity on the Church of England overturned the delicate equilibrium that James had carefully nurtured, and unleashed bitter hostility that contributed significantly to the events leading to the outbreak of civil war in 1642.

Questions

1. To what extent, if at all, did the years 1618–1625 see a change in James's religious policies compared with the period up to 1618?
2. In what ways do the 'British' and European contexts help to explain the successes and failures of James's religious policies?

SOURCES

1. JAMES AND THE PURITANS

Source A: From the Millenary Petition, presented to James in April 1604.

We the ministers of the gospel in this land, neither as factious men affecting a popular parity in the Church, nor as schismatics aiming at the dissolution of the state ecclesiastical; but as the faithful servants of Christ, and loyal subjects to your Majesty, desiring and longing for the redress of divers abuses of the Church ... [request] ...

I. ... That the cross in baptism ... may be taken away; ... the cap and surplice not urged ...
II. ... That none hereafter be admitted into the ministry but able and sufficient men; and those to preach diligently ... that non-residency be not permitted ...
III. ... that double-beneficed men be not suffered to hold some two, some three benefices with cure, and some two, three, or four dignities besides.

Source B: From James's reply to John Knewstubb on the final day of the Hampton Court Conference, 18 January 1604.

You show yourself an uncharitable man; we have here taken pains and in the end have concluded of a unity and uniformity, and you forsooth [in truth] must prefer the credits of a few private men before the general peace of the Church . . . I will none of that . . . and therefore, either let them conform themselves, and that shortly, or they shall hear of it.

Source C: From the Canons of the Church of England, September 1604.

   VI. Whoever shall hereafter affirm that the rites and ceremonies of the Church of England by law established are wicked, anti-Christian, or superstitious . . . let him be excommunicated . . .

  VII. Whoever shall hereafter affirm that the government of the Church of England under his Majesty by archbishops, bishops, deans, archdeacons . . . is anti-Christian and repugnant to the Word of God, let him be excommunicated . . .

XXXVI. No person shall hereafter be received into the ministry . . . except he shall first subscribe to these three articles following . . .

   (I) That the King's Majesty, under God, is the only supreme governor of this realm . . . as well in all spiritual or ecclesiastical things or causes as temporal . . .

  (II) That the Book of Common Prayer, and of ordering of bishops, priests and deacons, containeth in it nothing contrary to the Word of God, and that . . . he himself will use the form in the said Book prescribed in public prayer and administration of the sacraments, and none other.

 (III) That he alloweth the [Thirty-Nine Articles] . . . to be agreeable to the Word of God.

Source D: From James's letter to Robert Carr, Earl of Somerset, early in 1615.

It hath ever been my common answer to any that would plead for favour to a Puritan minister by reason of his rare gifts, that I had rather have a conformable man with but ordinary parts than the rarest men in the world that will not be obedient, for that leaven of pride sours the whole loaf.

Source E: Owen Felltham on Puritans, c. 1623.

I find many that are called Puritans, yet few, or none that will own the name. Whereof the reason sure is this, that 'tis for the most part held a name of infamy;

and is so new, that it hath scarcely yet obtained definition … So that I believe there are men that would be Puritans; but indeed not any that are. One will have him that lives religiously … Another, him that separates from our divine assemblies. Another, him that in some tenets only is peculiar. Another, him that will not swear. Absolutely to define him is a work, I think, of difficulty.

Questions

1. (i) Read Source A. What was the significance of the request that 'the cap and surplice be not urged'? [2]
   (ii) Read Source E. Comment on the phrase 'him that will not swear'. [2]
2. How far do Sources B and C indicate that Source A had failed to achieve its purpose? [5]
3. How far do Sources B, C and D show James pursuing a consistent policy towards Puritans? [5]
4. How useful is Source E as evidence of the nature and extent of Puritanism by 1623? [4]
*5. Use these sources and your own knowledge to assess how far, and by what means, James succeeded in winning over Puritan critics of the Church of England. [7]

Worked answer

*5. *[It is important to analyse James's methods as well as to evaluate his success, showing how the Sources fit into the wider picture.]*

James sought to win over Puritan critics of the Church of England by a mixture of conciliation and firmness. He went some way towards meeting the demands they had made in the Millenary Petition, for example by taking steps to reduce absenteeism and pluralism among the clergy and by commissioning a new translation of the Bible. The 1604 Canons acknowledged Puritan lecturers or preachers, and also permitted the 'prophesyings' (preaching) that Elizabeth I had forbidden.

At the same time, James made it clear that he expected all clergy and ministers to accept certain basic tenets. In particular, as Source C shows, they were required to accept the structure and doctrine of the established Church and to recognise the royal supremacy. Puritans were expected to conform outwardly. James refused to let the interests 'of a few private men' disrupt 'the general peace of the Church' (Source B). Obedience was essential for the preservation of order within the Church (Source D). Only those who flagrantly refused to conform, or who posed a political threat to the royal supremacy, suffered penalties. Puritans who accepted the basic framework of the Church and did not threaten its stability were granted a considerable degree of latitude in the precise details of worship.

James also encouraged a climate in which beliefs and practices were defined as little as possible. As Source E indicates, the term 'Puritan' remained vague and poorly defined, allowing many Puritans to be absorbed within the Church.

In general, Puritans were able to live with the Jacobean Church. Very few boycotted it completely. They regarded James as a godly prince who was moving the Church in the right direction, albeit too slowly. It was to be a very different story during the reign of Charles I.

SOURCES

2. JAMES AND THE CATHOLICS

Source F: From James's letter to Henry Percy, Earl of Northumberland, 24 March 1603.

As for the Catholics, I will neither persecute any that will be quiet and give but an outward obedience to the law, neither will I spare to advance any of them that will by good service worthily deserve it.

Source G: From the Oath of Allegiance, imposed on James's Catholic subjects in 1606.

I, A.B., do truly and sincerely acknowledge, profess, testify and declare in my conscience before God and the world, that our sovereign Lord King James is lawful and rightful king of this realm and of all other his Majesty's dominions and countries, and that the pope ... hath [no] power or authority to depose the king ... I will bear faith and true allegiance to his Majesty, his heirs and successors ... And I do further swear, that I do from my heart abhor, detest and abjure as impious and heretical this damnable doctrine and position that princes which be excommunicated and deprived by the pope may be deposed or murdered by their subjects or any other whatsoever.

Source H: From James's Directions to Preachers, sent to Archbishop Abbot on 4 August 1622.

V. That no preacher ... shall presume causelessly (and without invitation from the text) to fall into bitter invectives and indecent railing speeches against the persons of either papists or Puritans, but modestly and gravely (when they are occasioned thereunto by the text of Scripture), free both the doctrine and discipline of the Church of England from the aspersions of either adversary.

Source I: From a letter from John Williams, Bishop of Lincoln and Lord Keeper, to James Hamilton, Earl of Arran, 17 September 1622.

This argument . . . that the King favoureth the popish religion is such a composition of folly and malice as is little deserved by that gracious prince, who by . . . all professions and endeavours in the world hath demonstrated himself so resolved a Protestant.

Questions

1. (i) Read Source F. Explain the significance of the phrase 'an outward obedience to the law'. [2]
   (ii) Read Source H. Comment on the phrase 'the aspersions of either adversary'. [2]
*2. How far does Source G confirm or contradict James's intention expressed in Source F? Use your own knowledge and the content of these Sources in your answer. [5]
3. How far do Sources F, G and H suggest that James's policy towards English Catholics was driven more by the needs of changing circumstances than by any consistent vision? [5]
4. How convincing do you find John Williams's assertions in Source I? [4]
5. Use these Sources and your own knowledge to assess how successfully James handled the English Catholic community. [7]

Worked answer

*2. *[It is important to assess how far, if at all, James's views in a private letter differed from those he revealed in public. Examine carefully how circumstances had changed between the writing of the two documents.]*

In one sense, Source G follows directly from James's general aim stated in Source F. In Source F, written very shortly before he learnt of his accession to the throne of England, he declares that he will not persecute Catholics provided that they demonstrate 'an outward obedience to the law'. The Oath of Allegiance in Source G is designed to enforce such an obedience. In particular, it reflects James's deep fears about papal claims to excommunicate and depose foreign rulers as heretics, and to absolve their subjects of any duty of obedience or allegiance. The oath thus required English Catholics explicitly to reject any such doctrine and to affirm their loyalty and obedience to the King.

Although broadly consistent, in another sense Source G went slightly beyond James's general position expressed in Source F. The Oath of Allegiance was a direct response to the Gunpowder Plot of November 1605, which dramatically revealed that certain Catholic extremists felt no obligation of allegiance to the King. Amid the Protestant outcry which followed, the imposition of such an oath was probably inevitable. James insisted that it should test political allegiance and not require Catholics to renounce their spiritual allegiance to the Pope. Yet it is likely that even this probed further into Catholic consciences than he had initially hoped, and it was a source of great disappointment to him that successive popes refused to approve of the oath.

3

JAMES I

Parliaments and finances

BACKGROUND NARRATIVE

In the early part of the seventeenth century Parliament remained, in the words of Conrad Russell, 'an event and not an institution'.[1] Indeed, over the course of the twenty-two years of James I's reign, Parliament was in session for only about thirty-six months. During the rest of the period James ruled according to his prerogative, the general term applied to royal discretionary powers. However, the ill-defined nature of these royal rights and privileges led to disagreements in each of James's Parliaments.

The monarch's main expectation from a Parliament was that it would provide money (supply), though it was also generally antici-pated that it would pass legislation and offer advice. Although James met with four Parliaments in England – 1604–1611, 1614, 1621 and 1624 – he received little money. Indeed, the percentage of total revenue derived from parliamentary taxation amounted to only about 9 per cent during this period. In part, this was because MPs were reluctant to grant money to a King who was plainly spendthrift, but also it was because of inadequacies in the system. Meanwhile, MPs used Parliament as a platform from which to articulate their griev-ances, the most potent of which in 1610 and 1614 was impositions – customs duties which the Crown could levy without consulting Parliament. In 1621 and 1624 distress over impositions was replaced by concern about patents and monopolies.

Of James's four Parliaments only the first possessed any longevity, finally collapsing over the Great Contract – a scheme to reform the royal finances. The Parliament of 1614 – known as the Addled Parliament because no legislation resulted from its sitting – was quickly dissolved because, among other things, it threatened to withhold supply unless James abandoned impositions. All went well during the first session of the 1621 Parliament but differing opinions as to how best to resolve the European crisis, and MPs' growing fears that their privileges were so in jeopardy that they needed some sort of protection, meant that it was dissolved with only the two subsidy acts having been passed.

Whatever the problems of its predecessors, James's final Parliament was in many ways a great success. In particular, a significant quantity of legislation was passed, including a Monopolies Act, the terms of which forbade the Crown from granting monopolies to individuals, a long-standing grievance of MPs.

ANALYSIS (1): WHAT CAUSED JAMES'S FINANCIAL DIFFICULTIES? WHY DID IT MATTER THAT THE CROWN WAS IN DEBT?

In 1620 the King's debt totalled about £900,000, a figure to which it had risen from £500,000 in 1613.

While it was widely recognised that, as the Lord Treasurer Salisbury reminded Parliament in 1610, 'for a King not to be bountiful were a fault', other contemporaries lamented of James that 'for thrift and saving, he could never be brought to think of them'.[2] Indeed, as early as 1591 James confessed to Chancellor Maitland that he had 'offended the whole country [i.e. Scotland] for prodigal giving'.[3] Thus, between 1603 and 1607 James gave away monetary gifts to the value of £68,153 and pensions worth almost £30,000 a year. A grand total of £185,000 was spent on jewels. Large sums were drunk up by Court entertainments, particularly masques – a ritualised blend of dance, drama and fantasy – and the building of a new banqueting house designed by Inigo Jones. The cost of running the royal household in 1611 stood at more than £100,000, up from £64,000 in the last year of Elizabeth's reign. At least £85,315 was lavished upon royal country houses between James's accession in 1603 and Michaelmas 1611. Upon the marriage of Princess Elizabeth to Frederick of the Palatinate in 1613, a total of £93,000 was deducted from the royal coffers, £9,000 of which was employed to stage a sham battle on the Thames. In the same year, when James's favourite, Rochester, married Frances Howard, Crown lands valued at £10,000 were sold in order to provide a gift of jewels for the bride.

Royal expenditure spiralled also because, unlike his predecessor, the King was obliged to maintain two other royal households apart from his own, one for the Queen, Anne of Denmark, and the other for the heir to the throne, Prince Henry. The latter cost a total of £35,765 in 1610–1611.

Debt continued to mount not only as a consequence of the 'continual haemorrhage of outletting' effected by the King but because of the impact of persistent and significant inflation, the effect of which had been to increase prices by about 500% during the course of the sixteenth century.[4] This was disastrous for the Crown because revenue it received from land, its largest source of income, was peculiarly difficult to adjust to inflation. Valuation of Crown estate for rental purposes was undertaken by local men who were often related to those resident on the estate being assessed. Consequently, under-assessment was commonplace. For instance, in Sussex the average sum at which seventy-eight families were assessed fell from £48 each in 1560 to £14 in 1626. The Duke of Buckingham was assessed at £400 even though his income was about £15,000 in 1623. In 1601 Sir Walter Raleigh observed that 'our estates that be £30 or £40 in the Queen's books are not the hundredth part of our wealth'.[5] As the yield from Crown lands duly diminished they were sold off, a process which raised capital but at the expense of reducing the total revenue from rents. Thus, yearly income from Crown lands dropped from £128,257 in 1603 to £95,430 in 1621. The sale of Crown land had been pursued aggressively by Elizabeth I who, rather than tackle the thorny problem of under-assessment, raised £339,000 by such means but even so managed to bequeath to her successor a debt of £400,000. Another consequence of under-assessment was that the value of a parliamentary subsidy fell dramatically from about £137,000 in 1558 to £70,000 in 1621. In real terms therefore the value of a subsidy to the Crown had decreased by 87 per cent since the reign of Henry VIII. Little wonder that a later Fifth Monarchist was moved to compare Good Queen Bess to 'a sluttish housewife, who swept the house but left the dust behind the door'.[6]

Yet to the vast majority of the political nation the adverse financial circumstances of the Crown during James's reign were a direct consequence of the extravagance of the King himself. This perception was important for two reasons in particular. First, MPs' abhorrence at James's extravagance not only deterred them from offering supply – 'for if the bottoms be out', argued one MP, 'then can they not be filled' – but bolstered them in their belief that during peacetime the monarch should 'live of his own'.[7] In other words, it was generally felt that James should rely upon income derived from his ordinary revenues – rents, feudal dues, profits from justice and customs duties. Only in exceptional circumstances, during times of war and in moments of national danger such as the Gunpowder Plot, did MPs consider it necessary to provide the monarch with extraordinary revenue, usually in the form of a subsidy. Indeed, Roger Lockyer has estimated that during the whole of James's reign the Crown received a total of £910,00 from parliamentary grants, an average of only £41,000 for each year – equivalent to about 8 per cent of the ordinary revenue. The maintenance of this distinction between ordinary and extraordinary revenues was a consequence of James's extravagance and did much to cause difficulties between Crown and Parliament in the early part of the seventeenth century.

Second, Jacobean extravagance served to obscure the deep structural problems inherent in the system which in turn inhibited the processes of reform. What was the point, argued many an MP, in reforming the public finance system if the consequence of any such reformation served only to facilitate James's profligacy, especially when royal largesse was showered upon the Scots at the expense of the English: between 1603 and 1610, Scottish beneficiaries in all gained on average £40,000 a year in gifts or pensions, whereas the English received only an annual average of £10,000. In 1614 Nicholas Hyde asserted that James had given away to one or two men 'more than Queen Elizabeth gave to all her servants and favourites in all her reign. If these excesses continue, it is impossible for the kingdom to subsist, or us to help it.'[8] Indeed, the Earl of Clarendon later claimed that James had given to one of his Scottish favourites, James Hay, a sum totalling £400,000 – equivalent to the entire Crown revenue in a single year.

A concern that they would be subsidising a spendthrift monarch was one of the reasons why MPs failed to support the Great Contract in 1610. This was a scheme devised by Salisbury to win for the Crown a one-off payment of £600,000 and thereafter an annual grant of £200,000 from Parliament in return for the Crown surrendering its feudal rights of wardship and purveyance – an ability to assume the guardianship of those of its tenants who inherited estates as minors, and to purchase transport, food and other supplies at prices well below market level. The failure of the Great Contract meant that, for all his success between 1618 and 1624 – saving £87,000 a year together with an annual increase in revenue of £37,000 – Lord Treasurer Cranfield could do no more than tinker with the system as it stood.

The failure to reform the public finances ensured that, as Russell has noted, 'whenever the English tried to do anything abroad, the whole constitutional and financial situation would come to a head'.[9] This was certainly the case in 1628 when, out of a disastrous attempt to fight France and Spain simultaneously, the Petition of Right was forged. Then, after Charles I had been defeated by the Scots in the Second Bishops' War, the unreformed financial system was of key importance in that the Crown's financial difficulties allowed opposition MPs to hold it to ransom while they dismantled key aspects of its prerogative.

Equally important was the political effect of the declining value of a subsidy combined with MPs' reluctance to offer supply, a set of circumstances which meant that the monarch had little incentive to call Parliaments and instead was encouraged to exploit non-parliamentary sources of revenue according to his prerogative powers. The result was a vicious circle in which frustration and mutual incomprehension mounted between Crown and Parliament and turned finance into the most vexatious issue of Jacobean parliamentary politics.

In part this was because some of the money-raising devices employed by the Crown were fundamentally objectionable to many. For instance, wardship – a source from which Salisbury managed to augment the Crown's income from £14,000 in 1603 to £23,000 in 1612 – created resentment because it allowed the Crown to exploit the ward's estates and even to fine the ward when he came of age. Thus, the Commons' Apology of 1604 had formally listed wardship and purveyance as grievances. Indeed, the extent to which these devices served to alienate many of the political nation can be seen from Salisbury's offer to have them abolished according to the terms of the Great Contract.

In 1611 the new title of baronet was created and put up for sale at £1,095. By 1614 this had brought in £90,885, a rate of success which encouraged the Crown to offer for sale in 1615 peerages at the price of £10,000 each. Lawrence Stone has estimated that between 1603 and 1629 a total of £620,000 was received by the Crown from the sale of honours.[10] However, as C. Durston has pointed out, 'this apparently painless revenue source did have some serious repercussions as it brought the Crown into disrespect and created some considerable animosity between the old and new peers'.[11]

In the Parliament of 1621 the Commons turned to investigate the royal grants of patents and monopolies which many blamed for the current economic crisis. This was delicate ground to tread, eventually leading to the revival of the medieval process of impeachment, a form of trial where the Lower House acted as prosecutors and the Upper as judge and jury. Its first victims were Sir Francis Michell and Sir Giles Mompesson, entrepreneurs who had benefited from being granted monopolies to license inns and to manufacture gold and silver thread, respectively. Since there was a pervasive belief that 'the King could do no wrong', the Commons turned upon those whom they perceived as responsible for the original grant of these monopolies. Though James warned the Houses not to 'abridge the authority of courts, nor my prerogative', he nevertheless allowed MPs successfully to pursue the process of impeachment.

By far the most successful of the fiscal feudal devices employed by the Crown was the levying of impositions, additional duties on imports which had received legal backing according to the judgement in Bate's Case in 1606. A revised Book of Rates in 1608 ensured that impositions brought in £70,000 in 1614, roughly the equivalent to a single subsidy. Conrad Russell, noting that there was a 'deafening' silence on the issue of impositions in the Parliaments of 1621 and 1624, has done much to argue that the debate over impositions did not become the focus for profound constitutional conflict during the reign of James.[12] Nevertheless, the efficiency of impositions meant that MPs became concerned that Parliaments would henceforth be called less frequently, perhaps even not at all. Arguments over impositions significantly contributed to the collapse of the 1614 Parliament without the passage of any legislation, the so-called Addled Parliament. 'So do our impositions increase in England as it is come to be almost a tyrannical government in England,' lamented Sir Edwin Sandys.[13] Moreover, James's insistence in 1610 that MPs should not question his right to levy impositions quickly broadened out into a debate about the privilege of free speech, a constitutional clash being narrowly avoided only because James offered the Commons concessions and pressure of events forced debates about the Great Contract to the fore.

Though James's financial difficulties were therefore by no means all of his own making, his extravagance made a bad situation worse and contributed to the tensions between Crown and Parliament.

Questions

1. How do you account for James's financial difficulties?
2. Examine the constitutional implications of James's spendthrift nature.

ANALYSIS (2): TO WHAT EXTENT IS IT POSSIBLE TO TALK OF THERE BEING A 'CRISIS OF PARLIAMENTS' DURING THE REIGN OF JAMES I?

Considering the lack of definition in the constitution in the early part of the seventeenth century it was always likely that there would occur disagreement about the practical relationships between Crown and Parliament and between the prerogative of the monarch and the privileges of the two Houses, the Commons and the Lords. Arguing that James tactlessly triggered debate about both the nature and origins of royal power and parliamentary privilege and the common law, Whig historians have alleged that the Commons, in order to preserve their liberties which they perceived to be under threat from James, went on to 'win the initiative' from the Crown.[14] Consequently, the disagreements between James and his Parliaments take the form of constitutional flashpoints, each of which marked a deepening crisis and in totality represented a historical escalator leading inevitably to civil war. However, more recently, it has been pointed out that on general issues of political theory a very high level of agreement existed between James and his subjects and that everyone subscribed to the same basic principles about the 'ancient constitution'. Above all, rather than provoking a 'crisis of Parliaments' because of his absolutist nature, it has been demonstrated that James possessed a marked ability to reconcile and restore harmony within the political nation.[15]

Nevertheless, at least upon first examination, it seems as though the Whig position is a compelling interpretation of events. For instance, an important reason for the Crown calling a Parliament was in order to seek the passage of particular pieces of legislation. However, even though James had let it be known that he was determined that his first Parliament (1604–1611) should advance the statutory union of England and Scotland so that he could bequeath 'one worship to God, one kingdom entirely governed, one uniformity in laws', the royal ambition met with bitter disappointment.[16] Centuries of English hatred of the Scots and a pervasive fear 'that the first hour wherein the Parliament gives the King the name of Great Britany, there follow necessarily . . . an utter extinction of all the laws now in force' meant that the Commons refused to consider any Act of Union.[17] By 1607–1608 the scheme was effectively dead, and James had only been able to assume the title of 'King of Great Britain' by issuing a royal proclamation in October 1604. The Commons appeared equally obstructive in their refusal to assent to the Great Contract – Salisbury's attempt in 1610 to effect fundamental reform of the Crown finances – even though James had offered concessions, a course of action which he viewed as 'without example of any king before'.[18]

Not only did the Commons apparently thwart the royal will but on a number of occasions it seemed as though they did indeed 'win the initiative' and, by so doing, induce a crisis in their relationship with the Crown. First, the Buckinghamshire election case of 1604 seemingly established unambiguously the right of the Commons to decide disputed elections and thereby prevent the Crown from 'packing' the House with those it knew it could rely on for support. Second, in 1621, for the first time since 1459, MPs made use of impeachment (see Analysis (1), above). In the Parliaments of 1621 and 1624 it was used against Crown servants, Lord Chancellor Sir Francis Bacon and Lord Treasurer Middlesex respectively. Third, in James's last Parliament, MPs ensured that the supply they voted was tied (appropriated) to specific items of expenditure, namely the navy, aid to the Dutch and defence of the British Isles. In each of these respects it seemed as though the prerogative of the Crown was being diminished vis-à-vis the influence and privileges sought by the Commons.

Moreover, the existence of a crisis seemed yet more real because, as argued by the Whigs, these events were played out against an apparent ideological struggle centring on MPs' insistence that they should enjoy certain privileges even if this meant invading the royal prerogative. For the majority of MPs the most important of their perceived privileges were freedom of speech and immunity from arrest while Parliament was sitting, the latter of which seemed in jeopardy after James had pronounced in December 1621 'that we think ourself very free and able to punish any man's misdemeanours in Parliament, as well during their sitting as after'.[19] Yet it was the Commons' claim to freedom of speech which had apparently already induced an atmosphere of crisis in the Jacobean Parliaments. As early as 1604 they had drawn up a defence of their position, the Form of Apology and Satisfaction, in which they protested that their privileges were integral to 'the rights and liberties of the whole commons of your realm of England which they and their ancestors from time immemorable have undoubtedly enjoyed'.[20] It is certainly the case that arguments over free speech were responsible for bringing the Parliament of 1621 to a peremptory conclusion. On that occasion, when MPs began to debate foreign policy – an aspect of government that was traditionally reserved to the Crown – James warned them not to 'presume henceforth to meddle with anything concerning our government or deep matters of state'.[21] Ultimately, in the Commons' Protestation of 18 December 1621, the House insisted that members had the right to discuss 'arduous and urgent affairs concerning the King, state, and defence of the realm, and of the Church of England'.[22] After this had been inscribed in the Commons' Journal, the King sent for that record of events, tore out the offending page and then dissolved Parliament. The meeting of a Parliament, an occasion which MPs and Crown alike had hitherto perceived as a point of contact, seemed to have become a point of friction.

Yet, meticulous attention to documentary detail has persuaded Conrad Russell to argue that 'before 1640 Parliament was not powerful and that it did not contain an opposition'.[23] From this it follows that there was no 'high road to civil war', a conclusion which in turn suggests that compromise was a more prevalent feature of Jacobean Parliaments than crisis.

Although this revisionist interpretation of events has not gone without criticism, it is no longer possible to perceive the Commons as 'winning the initiative' and thereby inducing a crisis in their relationship with the Crown.[24] Not least, by indicating that James was by no means a tyrannical King aiming to fashion an absolute form of government, recent research has removed the reason for the Commons wanting to win the initiative. For instance, a new analysis of the Buckinghamshire election case of 1604 shows that James acted with moderation and in a conciliatory fashion, conceding of his own free will that the Commons were indeed a court of record and the proper judge of election returns. 'Certainly there is no real evidence', concludes R. C. Munden, 'that this affair unduly soured relations between King and Commons'.[25]

Nor was there any sense of a constitutional paralysis upon the failure of the Great Contract. It failed not only because of the intransigence of MPs but because James himself became wary about giving up purveyance and wardship in return for an annual sum whose value would soon be eroded by inflation. Even the failure of the union is no longer seen as evidence for the collapse of the parliamentary process. Jenny Wormald has recently argued that James's quest for a statutory union with Scotland was not his final bargaining position, but an extreme one which allowed him room for manoeuvre. 'Anything less than the creation of the British identity which the King appeared to desire so ardently would look like gain to its English opponents', an outcome which made it much less politically difficult for James to achieve another objective, the retention of large numbers of Scots at Court.[26]

Also, the detail of events shows that there was in no sense an organised opposition party in the Houses motivated consistently by some deep-seated ideological prejudice. Even the question of free speech was much less of a point of conflict than the Whigs alleged. For instance, the Apology of 1604 was much more concerned with financial issues than free speech. It was also drawn up by a minority of MPs, was never adopted by the Commons as a whole, and was never presented to James. Strikingly, in 1624, with his reaction to the Protestation seemingly forgotten, James opened Parliament with a request that MPs should give him their 'advice in matters of greatest weight and importance'.[27] Though it is true, for example, that resentment in the Commons at the Crown's use of impositions did much to sour events in 1610 and 1614, thereafter, as Russell has observed, there is only a deafening silence on this issue.[28] Moreover, it is now apparent that opposition which did occur took the form of ever-changing factions that came together from time to time to champion a particular cause and were often mobilised and led by elements within the Privy Council. Thus, impeachment was employed by Privy Councillors as a power tool to remove their enemies rather than by the Commons against the advisers of the Crown.

Therefore, aspects of Jacobean Parliaments which to the Whigs were representative of some deep crisis now appear as commonplace in the proceedings of an early modern assembly, more akin to the gradual, unfelt and everyday shifting of the plates of the earth rather than dramatic and convulsive volcanic eruptions.

However, the Commons failed to function at all efficiently in one very important respect: the provision of supply. In total, James received just over £900,000 from parliamentary grants – equivalent to about 8 per cent of the ordinary revenue collected by the Crown over the course of the reign. As Russell puts it, it was 'hard to see what, in financial terms, [the King] stood to gain from calling future Parliaments'.[29] In short, 'the English Parliament before 1629 was heading for extinction'.[30]

Increasingly, therefore, the Crown was obliged to raise money by its prerogative devices, above all impositions. This antagonised the Commons because it was taxation without their assent and thus diminished their ability to obtain redress of grievances, an expectation which most voters placed upon their MP. Indeed, only in 1614 did the Commons even attempt to obtain a redress of grievances by withholding supply, an action for which they were peremptorily dissolved.

Clearly, all was not well in the Parliaments of James but to describe the difficulties that occurred as amounting to a 'crisis' is to go too far. Furthermore, in some respects Parliament continued to function as expected. There was, for instance, no decrease in Parliament's capacity to pass legislation. The five parliamentary sessions of 1604–1611 produced no fewer than 226 acts and, though the Parliament of 1621 produced only two, there were over fifty in preparation when it was dissolved. The Parliament of 1624 produced seventy-three acts, prompting Hirst to describe this as 'a testimonial to harmony'.[31] Moreover, as a point of contact, Parliament remained as significant as ever to the King and members of the political nation, important to the latter because their social standing in the localities depended upon their attendance at Westminster, and important to the former because the Crown continued to rely upon the unpaid services of the political nation to impose its will in the country. Nevertheless, moments of temporary conflict which had been a feature of Parliaments during the reign of James could harden into periods of prolonged crisis given a change of circumstance. In 1625 that change was profound: a new monarch, engaged in war.

Questions

1. Examine the claim that Parliament was 'winning the initiative' during the reign of James I.
2. To what extent were the difficulties in Parliaments during the reign of James I a consequence of the inadequacy of the King himself?

SOURCES

1. JACOBEAN FINANCES

Source A: A letter from Matthew Hutton, Archbishop of York, to Lord Cecil, 10 August 1604.

His Majesty's subjects hear and fear that his excellent and heroical nature is too much inclined to giving, which in short will exhaust the treasure of this kingdom and bring many inconveniences.

Source B: Part of the *Poor Man's Petition to the King at Theobalds*, 17 April 1603.

Good King . . . A plague upon all covetous Treasurers! Good King, look to thy Takers and Officers of the House, and to their exceeding fees, that peele and powle [i.e. tax] thy Princely allowance.

Source C: A letter from the Lord Treasurer, the Earl of Dorset, to Sir Julius Caesar, not dated but endorsed by Caesar on 9 June 1607.

You may answer [i.e. to those that petition you for money] that the King's debts, his subsidies, his rents, his revenues, notwithstanding all the means of levying of them that possibly may be devised, are not paid, but piecemeal come in with great difficulty ... Besides his Majesty hath brought with him an increase of a most comfortable charge; as of a Queen ... a Prince; and other his most royal progeny.

Source D: A letter from John More to Secretary Winwood, 1 December 1610.

I conceive by the common discourse that the Parliament could be content to replenish the royal cistern (as they call it) of His Majesty's Treasury, were they assured that His Majesty's largess to the Scots' prodigality would not cause a continual and remedy-less leak therein.

Source E: Lionel Cranfield's notes for a speech to Parliament, November 1621. (Cranfield, Earl of Middlesex, headed the Treasury Commission 1621–1624.)

[Whenever did] the people of England live eighteen years together in such peace and plenty with so little charge to [i.e. by] their King as they have done since his Majesty's reign ... The people not withstanding all this improvement to their estates, never since the Conquest gave so little to the King ... as they have done to his Majesty.

Questions

1. Read Source C.
   (i) What were 'subsidies'? [2]
   (ii) Apart from subsidies and rents, give two other examples of royal 'revenues'. [2]
2. What reasons do these Sources put forward to explain the 'growing and great necessities' of James? [6]
3. Considering Dorset's position and responsibilities, why might a historian using Source C be suspicious of the explanation it provides for James's financial difficulties? [3]
4. Read Source E. How effective do you consider Cranfield's speech as part of a request for Parliament to meet the King's financial needs? [5]
*5. Use these Sources and your own knowledge to consider the notion that James's financial difficulties were the inevitable consequence of a financial system that was out of date and difficult to reform rather than the fact that the King was 'too much inclined to giving'. [7]

Worked answer

*5. *[Having briefly acknowledged 'James's financial difficulties', it is important to recognise that there are two main parts to this question,* *each of which should receive roughly equal treatment. It is also important that the response argue a case illustrated with examples directly dependent on the content of the Sources and knowledge obtained from wider reading.]*

Throughout his reign James I was in significant debt, a circumstance which provided for difficulties in his relations with Parliament.

There is much evidence to support the notion that the 'financial system was out of date'. Even in the early seventeenth century the majority of the political nation adhered to the medieval belief that the Crown should 'live of its own' during times of peace, a philosophy which partly explains why only about 9 per cent of total revenue derived from parliamentary taxation during James's reign. Cranfield was correct to lament that 'the people . . . gave so little to the King' (Source E). But this situation was also a consequence of inflation, ensuring that by the end of James's reign the value of a subsidy had decreased by about 87 per cent since the reign of Henry VIII. It was difficult for the Crown to tackle this problem because in the absence of a trained, salaried civil service it was forced to rely upon the goodwill of the political nation in order to collect taxes, a system which invited corruption. Indeed, Source B comments upon 'covetous Treasurers' and 'Takers . . . of the House'. Moreover, under-assessment became commonplace and, as Source C indicates, many of the Crown revenues came in 'piecemeal' and 'with great difficulty'.

The King was indeed 'too much inclined to giving'. For example, between 1603 and 1607 James gave away monetary gifts to the value of £68,153 and pensions worth almost £30,000 a year. His extravagance led to a number of 'inconveniences' (Source A), not least of which was a reluctance by MPs to reform a system merely to sustain a 'continual haemorrhage of outletting'.

Thus, the two main parts of the statement cannot easily be separated. As Source D suggests, Parliament 'could' provide the King with more revenue if he ended his 'largess to the Scots' prodigality'. His failure to do so, along with the nature of the system he inherited and the conservative instinct of most MPs meant that reform proposals were few and far between and that the only one to come anywhere near success – namely, the Great Contract – was ultimately doomed.

SOURCES

2. PARLIAMENTS AND THE ROYAL PREROGATIVE

Source F: Form of Apology and Satisfaction, 20 June 1604.

What cause we your poor Commons have to watch over our privileges is manifest in itself to all men. The prerogatives of princes may easily and do daily grow; the privileges of the subject are for the most part at an everlasting stand.

Source G: From a speech by James to the Lords and Commons, 21 March 1610.

The state of Monarchy is the supremest thing upon earth for Kings are not only God's Lieutenants upon earth, and sit upon God's throne, but even by God himself they are called Gods ... In the Scriptures Kings are called Gods, and so their power after a certain relation compared to the Divine power. Kings are also compared to Fathers of families, for a King is truly ... the politic father of his people ... [But the King is bound] by a double oath to the fundamental Laws of his kingdom: tacitly, as by being a King, and so bound to protect as well the people as the Laws of his Kingdom; and expressly, by his oath at his coronation ... And therefore a King governing in a settled Kingdom leaves to be a King and degenerates into a Tyrant as soon as he leaves off to rule according to his Laws.

Source H: From the King's speech to both Houses, 5 April 1614.

Although there have been many speeches given abroad that the King would stretch his prerogative, like other of my predecessors, I never meant it. For he that overmuch strains and blows his nose will cause much blood. So, if a prince should stretch his prerogative, it would cause his people to bleed.

Source I: James's remarks to Gondomar, the Spanish envoy at the royal Court, after the dissolution of the Addled Parliament, 1614.

The House of Commons is a body without a head. The members give their opinion in a disorderly manner. At their meetings nothing is heard but cries, shouts and confusion. I am surprised that my ancestors should ever have permitted such an institution to come into existence. I am a stranger, and found it here when I arrived, so that I am obliged to put up with what I cannot get rid of.

Source J: The Commons' Petition, 9 December 1621.

And whereas your Majesty doth seem to abridge us of the ancient liberty of parliament for freedom of speech ..., a liberty which we assure ourselves so wise and so just a king will not infringe, the same being our ancient and undoubted right and an inheritance received from our ancestors.

Questions

*1. Explain what you understand by 'prerogatives of princes' and 'the privileges of the subject' referred to in Source F. [4]
2. To what extent are the concerns expressed in Source F supported by the detail of Sources G, H and I? [6]
3. With reference to the tone and language of each, which of the Sources H and J makes the more effective appeal? [5]
4. How useful is Source G to the historian researching the leadership abilities of James? [4]
5. 'The prerogatives of princes may easily and do daily grow.' Use these Sources and your own knowledge to assess to what extent this remark is an accurate reflection upon the reign of James I. [6]

Worked answer

*1. [Since this is a straightforward factual question which carries four marks you should aim to give four examples.]

As articulated by MPs in Jacobean Parliaments, 'privileges of the subject' is probably a reference to freedom of speech and immunity from arrest while Parliament is sitting. Amongst other things, 'prerogatives of princes' included the royal ability to call, prorogue and dissolve Parliaments at will.

4

BUCKINGHAM AND FOREIGN POLICY, 1618–1628

BACKGROUND NARRATIVE

In late 1614 and early 1615 it was clear to most observers that Robert Carr, Earl of Somerset, the favourite of James since 1612, would henceforth no longer enjoy the favours of the King. A victim of the intense factional rivalry that was a feature of all early modern Courts, he was replaced by a young man of twenty-two years whom one contemporary described as having 'delicate and handsome features [and whose] hands and face seemed to me especially effeminate and curious' and whom James came to refer to as his 'Sweet Steenie gossip' and 'Sweet child and wife'.[1] Yet George Villiers proved to be far more than either a plaything of King James or a conduit of a Court faction. By about 1619 he had emerged as what was effectively first minister. Showered with honours, he was ultimately created Duke of Buckingham in 1623 – the first duke for nearly a century to have no trace of royal blood in his veins. It was at this time that Buckingham ingratiated himself with Prince Charles, not least by accompanying the heir to the throne on an expedition to Spain in a failed attempt to win the hand of a Catholic Spanish princess, the Infanta.

It is a demonstration of Buckingham's considerable political agility that not only did he maintain his position after the accession of Charles in 1625 but that he proceeded to convince the new monarch that he was indispensable to the good government of the nation. However, as early as 1626 many contemporaries thought precisely the opposite, and one of them, a disaffected soldier called John Felton, stabbed Buckingham to death at Portsmouth on 23 August 1628.

Buckingham's shadow therefore looms large over the history of the 1620s, especially so in the Parliament of 1626 and, to a lesser extent, those of 1621, 1625 and the first session of the Parliament called in 1628. Yet the shadow he cast is made even darker, and events yet more complicated, by the impact of events abroad. The Palatinate crisis of 1618 (see page 57) eventually destroyed James's attempts to marry his son to the Infanta and, helped by the actions of Charles and Buckingham, culminated in England going to war against Spain in 1625. What is more difficult to fathom is why, from 1627, England was also engaged in hostilities with France, the enemy of Spain.

ANALYSIS (1): ASSESS THE EXTENT TO WHICH THE DUKE OF BUCKINGHAM WORSENED RELATIONS BETWEEN THE EARLY STUART KINGS AND THEIR SUBJECTS.

Before the advent of the revisionist historians an answer to this question would have been fairly easily constructed since most writers believed that the early Stuart period represented a 'high road to civil war', fashioned in part by the character and career of George Villiers, Duke of Buckingham. As such he deserved outright condemnation. '[The Duke] must rank amongst the most incapable ministers of this or any other country', concluded S. R. Gardiner.[2] H. R. Trevor-Roper held that Buckingham possessed 'a political megalomania which was a political disaster'.[3] Clayton Roberts remarked that 'governed by pride and passion . . . devoid of wisdom and prudence, [Buckingham] rushed from one disaster to another . . . His follies were not trivial, occasional or of a kind that can be explained away. They were continual, gross and palpable.'[4] However, in line with more recent interpretations which have stressed how little ideological division developed during these years, the career of Buckingham has enjoyed a rehabilitation. For instance, Conrad Russell has argued that Buckingham 'showed more sagacity than he has been given credit for'.[5] Here was a statesman more significant and more talented than historians hitherto have been willing to allow. Yet by far the most favourable reinterpretation of Buckingham to date is that offered by Roger Lockyer. In his biography of the Duke published in 1981, Lockyer argues that far from being an impediment to efficient government Buckingham was an effective reformer, as is evidenced, for example, by his support, until 1624, for Lord Treasurer Cranfield. Lockyer also asserts that the Duke pursued a coherent foreign policy. 'There was not a great deal wrong with Buckingham's policies', writes Lockyer, 'other than the lack of money with which to carry them into effect.'[6]

Nevertheless, it is clear that Buckingham was at least in part responsible for the fractiousness that afflicted some of the Parliaments of the 1620s. As noted by J. P. Kenyon:

> Buckingham's policy of selling peerages on a large scale, raising the numbers in the House [from 81 in 1615] to 126 by 1628, was a disaster. The older peers were enraged with the King and his advisers, and the loyalty of the new peers could not be relied on, with the result that in 1621, 1626 and 1628 the Lords joined the Commons in inflicting heavy defeats on James I and Charles I.[7]

Similarly, the extraordinary range of the favourite's patronage, extending into the judicial as well as the administrative sphere, had important political repercussions. Those who did not enjoy the goodwill of the favourite could not hope to prosper and were therefore driven to articulate their resentment in Parliament. Notable among such men was the Earl of Southampton who, in the first session of the Parliament of 1621, had worked closely with the Commons in order to promote attacks upon Buckingham. During the recess the Earl duly found himself arrested, an event which contributed to the souring of relations during the second session and raised MPs' fears about their privileges. Frustrated courtiers could also be driven to unprecedented activity in Parliaments if their standing in their county was placed under threat by their being denied Court patronage, a circumstance perhaps best illustrated by the feud between the two Yorkshiremen, Sir John Savile and Sir Thomas Wentworth. Having failed in his efforts to ingratiate himself with the Duke and alarmed at the way in which Savile was exploiting his position, Wentworth attached himself to the opposition. In particular, the latter's support for the Petition of Right in 1628 was probably designed in order to advertise his abilities to the Court, thereby winning favour and thus restoring his position in his locality.

Yet gentry alienation from the regime was limited because the disaffected were usually able to find friends at Court. Moreover, Russell has demonstrated that what resentment there was 'had very little ideological tinge to it' and, considering the wide spectrum of political and religious opinion patronised by Buckingham, concludes that 'it is hard to see how those who wished to be effective politicians could have entered into opposition to "the court" as a whole'.[8] However, Russell's thesis has not been accepted by all historians, particularly when it is applied to the late

1620s. By that time so great was the extent to which Buckingham had established a stranglehold over patronage that these historians have argued that the political nation had become polarised along a Court–country axis.[9]

Buckingham was certainly increasingly distrusted by the majority of the political nation, not least because of his association with Catholics and high churchmen, or anti-Calvinists. Increasingly he was suspected of being sympathetic to the anti-Calvinist element, becoming friendly with William Laud in the early 1620s and allowing one of his chaplains to preach what was described as an Arminian sermon at Cambridge in 1622. This suspicion was confirmed when Buckingham firmly identified himself with the anti-Calvinists at the York House debates in February 1626. This event, observes Lockyer,

> marked the end of the alliance between Buckingham . . . and the 'Protestant interest' – an alliance which, even though it had not prevented the attack upon the favourite in the Parliament of 1625, had served to restrain his enemies within certain bounds. The restraints were now removed, with consequences that became all too apparent in the ensuing session.[10]

Attacks upon Buckingham were inspired also by the knowledge that his mother had recently converted to Catholicism and that Katherine, his wife, was Catholic until her marriage – facts that to many observers placed the favourite at the centre of some sort of popish plot.

Not only was the Duke distrusted for religious reasons but, and increasingly, many of the political nation felt that he was advancing his own interests at the expense of the well-being of the common-wealth. When Prince Charles and Buckingham journeyed to Madrid in 1623, ostensibly to conclude the Spanish marriage, many held the favourite responsible for this extraordinarily hazardous expedition and protested at what they believed was a scheme designed solely to provide Buckingham with the opportunity to insinuate himself with the heir to the throne. Evidence suggests that the favourite had already engineered the sudden dissolution of the 1621 Parliament – encouraging an invasion of the royal prerogative which culminated in the Commons' resolution that 'our most noble prince may be timely and happily married to one of our own religion' – in order to stunt an apparently growing body of opinion which regarded him as 'the only author of all grievances and oppressions whatsoever'.[11]

Yet for a while in 1624 Buckingham effectively appeased his critics by espousing the very policy which most MPs wanted to hear – a determination to prosecute a naval war with Spain. In order to coerce

James into breaking off the Spanish marriage negotiations, Buckingham and Charles organised a 'patriot' coalition of MPs in the Parliament of 1624 which ensured a grant of £300,000 on the understanding that the money would be administered by a Council of War accountable to Parliament. They also co-operated with MPs to remove by impeachment Lord Treasurer Cranfield, an obstacle to war because he objected to its cost. Arguably, therefore, Buckingham was responsible for improving the Crown's relations with the political nation, not the opposite!

Yet for two reasons in particular his actions amounted to a dangerous strategy. First, as James observed, by manipulating Parliament the Duke was 'making a rod with which you will be scourged yourself'.[12] Second, by putting himself at the head of a body of popular opinion Buckingham was more than ever likely to be the scapegoat if things went wrong.

James's prediction came true. During the course of the two years following James's death in 1625, MPs' hostility once again focused on Buckingham, culminating in an attempt by the Parliament of 1626 to impeach the royal favourite. This change in the political atmosphere is explained in large part by the disastrous course of Caroline (from Carolus, Charles) foreign policy. There was no glorious sea war, expected by MPs, which harked back to the glory days of Elizabeth and which MPs expected. Instead, in January 1625 an expedition led by the German freebooter Mansfeld designed to relieve the Palatinate got no further than Flushing, a disaster which was followed in the autumn of 1625 by an expedition to Cadiz which met with similar ignominious failure. As Lord High Admiral and royal favourite, Buckingham was inextricably associated with these calamities. Indeed, as part of his quest to build an anti-Habsburg league the Duke had been instrumental in arranging the marriage, in 1625, of Charles to Henrietta Maria of France. However, Richelieu, the machiavellian French minister, had insisted upon terms which meant that this Anglo-French alliance was dangerously inconsistent with the outlook of the English Parliament. In particular, he had coerced Charles and Buckingham into providing for the suspension of recusancy laws, the release from prison of all Catholics and the loaning of English ships to help put down a rebellion of French Protestants, known as Huguenots, in La Rochelle. In order to obtain supply Buckingham would have to appease Parliament but by doing so he would disaffect the French. If he sought to fulfil the terms of the alliance he would disaffect Parliament and thereby obtain either no supply or supply that was insufficient to furnish an army or fleet. In his simultaneous pursuit of these incompatible aims Buckingham achieved nothing, except to arouse the suspicion and distrust of MPs and to ensure that from 1627 England was at war with France as well as Spain.

When it became clear that the Commons elected in 1626 would not vote any subsidies until Buckingham was 'removed from intermeddling with the great affairs of state', Charles dissolved Parliament in order to protect his favourite.[13] The consequences of this were twofold. First, those who had opposed the Duke were dismissed from the Court and replaced by men like the Earls of Rutland, Holland and Dorset who had emerged as his defenders. The effect of this was to diminish the role of the Court as a 'point of contact'. The Venetian Ambassador thus reported that many could not 'endure that one born a simple gentleman ... should be the sole access to the Court, the sole means of favour, in fact one might say the King himself'.[14] Second, desperate for finance to service the continuing war effort and encouraged by Buckingham and his supporters, the King now resorted to a number of extra-parliamentary devices to raise revenue, by far the most effective of which was the Forced Loan of 1627. While not denying that the Crown possessed the prerogative ability to raise money in this way, critics of the loan asserted that such a tax could be raised only in an emergency which, they claimed, did not exist at that time. At the very moment that the political nation was thus becoming dangerously polarised, Buckingham, in an attempt to win back the favour of Parliament, personally led an expedition to La Rochelle designed to help the Huguenots. It met with utter disaster. 'Since England was England, it received not so dishonourable a blow,' remarked one observer.[15] Such complete failure only served to heighten political tension and induce yet greater instability.

Ominously for the Crown, one of the effects of the Kings' support for Buckingham was that by the late 1620s the opposition was obliged to make its resistance more effective through planning and organisation. This came to fruition in the first session of the Parliament called in 1628 when, in return for a grant of five subsidies, MPs coerced the King into assenting to the Petition of Right. Having left off attacking Buckingham until the King had given his assent to the Petition, MPs now prepared a Remonstrance against the Duke and passed a resolution that 'the excessive power of the Duke of Buckingham, and the abuse of that power, are the chief cause of these evils and dangers to the King and kingdom'.[16] Yet, as one MP recorded, 'it is certain that His Majesty's favour to the Duke is in no way diminished', adding that 'the ill will of the people is like to be thereby much increased'.[17]

There is therefore no doubt that Buckingham did indeed worsen relations between the early Stuart kings and their subjects, partly as a consequence of his stranglehold on patronage, partly because of his attachment to the anti-Calvinists and partly because of his disastrous foreign policy. Yet other factors also explain these poor relations, especially the accession of Charles I in 1625, a King who, as John Reeve has observed, lacked 'political sense' and 'had no conception of the art of the possible'.[18]

Charles deepened the mistrust which bedevilled relations with his Parliaments by his readiness to resort to authoritarian and dubious methods. Thus, when the judges in the Five Knights' case in 1627 returned a verdict which was unsatisfactory to Charles he duly ordered the Attorney-General to change the judges' ruling into the one that he had originally sought. This was an extraordinary action because it brought into question the royal attitude towards the common law, as did the confiscation of the property of a number of London merchants, including John Rolle, in July 1628 upon their refusal to pay tonnage and poundage on the grounds that its collection had not been sanctioned by Parliament. 'Like King John,' notes J. P. Kenyon, 'King Charles was probing the wall of law and custom which protected his subjects' money in the hope of finding the odd gap through which he could press.'[19]

Charles's reputation for duplicity and subterfuge was enhanced by his attitude and actions during the passage of the Petition of Right. Not only did the King fail in the first instance to provide the traditional response to the Petition, thereby encouraging MPs to believe that he was considering a breach of faith, but, when the Petition came to be printed, he ordered that the statute number originally assigned to it be removed, thus making its authority as a statute much less certain.

Similarly, Charles rode roughshod over what MPs regarded as one of their fundamental privileges – freedom of arrest while Parliament was sitting. The incarceration of leading opponents of Buckingham – namely Sir Dudley Digges and Sir John Eliot in the Commons and the Earl of Arundel in the Lords – in the middle of the 1626 Parliament provided genuine cause for dismay. Indeed, in what proved a successful policy designed to secure the release of these men, the Commons suspended their sittings indefinitely while the Lords resolved on a week's cessation of business. The royal decision to appoint as sheriffs – and thereby deny the opportunity to stand for election – men such as Wentworth and Coke who had advertised their opposition to Buckingham in 1625 also backfired awkwardly because, as Kenyon has observed, this 'left the field open for personal enemies of Buckingham like Sir John Eliot, who wanted nothing better than to head a crusade against him'.[20]

Made taciturn by his stutter – indeed, observers referred to his 'reserved silence' – it was unfortunate that the King found no other means to explain such actions.[21] In an extraordinarily hamfisted manoeuvre, Charles enhanced the difficulties he and Buckingham faced. At a time when opinion in Parliament was already sensitive because of an informed realisation that there was an on-going retreat of representative assemblies on the continent, Sir Dudley Carleton delivered a speech on behalf of Charles to the Parliament of 1626. He told his listeners that:

> in all Christian kingdoms you know that parliaments were in use anciently . . . until the monarchs began to know their own strength, and, seeing the turbulent spirit of their parliaments, at length they little by little began to stand upon their prerogatives, and at last overthrew the parliaments throughout Christendom, except here only with us. . . . Let us be careful then to preserve the King's good opinion of parliaments.[22]

Meanwhile, Charles's attachment to the anti-Calvinists fomented a serious escalation of religious differences. Indeed, whereas Jacobean Parliaments had been noticeable for their absence of religious debate, much time in the early Parliaments of Charles was given over to this issue. MPs were alarmed when, after they had attacked the anti-Calvinist Richard Montagu in 1625 on the grounds that his writings 'tended to the disturbance of church and state', Charles appointed him a royal chaplain.[23] Their concern was deepened in 1627 following a number of sermons by anti-Calvinists justifying the King's decision to raise taxes without reference to Parliament. Two sermons in favour of the Forced Loan preached by Roger Manwaring in July 1627 made him the subject of an impeachment in 1628, though thereafter he was pardoned, advanced and made a royal chaplain by Charles. Similarly galling to MPs was the nomination of Montagu as Bishop of Chichester in 1628. Other anti-Calvinists were advanced at this time, notably William Laud as Bishop of London. A dangerous polarisation was thus becoming visible in the Church.

It is clear that any explanation of the difficulties suffered by James and Charles must give substantial consideration to the role of Buckingham. On the other hand, by no means all of the factors which contributed to poor relations between the early Stuart kings and their subjects were of the Duke's own making. There is no doubt that he was unlucky to have had to face the unsettling effects of a 'decay of trade', plague and a coterie of particularly 'fiery spirits' in the Commons, epitomised by Sir John Eliot. Moreover, this was a political nation which proved as consistently reluctant to finance war as it was persistent in calling for that eventuality, an aspect of what some historians have chosen to call a functional breakdown of government. Above all, though there is no denying that Buckingham became a monumental obstruction to good relations, this was more a consequence of the fact that he served a King who was flawed and less a result of his own inadequacies – a thesis demonstrated no more vividly than by the realisation that after the Duke had been murdered in August 1628 the problems in the second session of the 1628–1629 Parliament became even more intractable than when he had been alive (see Chapter 5).

Questions

1. In what ways, and for what reasons, was government of England difficult in the 1620s?
2. 'A political disaster' or a figure who 'showed more sagacity than he has been given credit for'? With which of these opinions of Buckingham do you agree? Explain your answer.

ANALYSIS (2): COMPARE AND CONTRAST THE FOREIGN POLICY OF JAMES VI AND I AND CHARLES I DURING THE PERIOD 1618–1630.

The early Stuarts, like their predecessors, regarded foreign policy as lying within the royal prerogative. Although this claim sometimes caused friction with their Parliaments, James and Charles nevertheless exerted considerable personal influence over the nature and conduct of foreign policy. International affairs in this period were often more a matter of personal relationships between royal dynasties than of relations between impersonal states, and the making of war or peace closely reflected the characters, beliefs and priorities of individual rulers. The differing personalities and political styles of James and Charles were thus plainly evident in their contrasting approaches to foreign policy.

James's foreign policy rested on two closely related ideals: to keep England at peace, and to foster international harmony and reconciliation, especially in religious matters. He saw himself as the peacemaker-king ('Rex Pacificus'), and took as his motto 'beati pacifici' ('blessed are the peacemakers'). Shortly after becoming King of England he signed the Treaty of London (August 1604), ending the war that had been fought against Spain since 1585. Thereafter, James regularly played the part of an international mediator, for example in promoting the Truce of Antwerp between Spain and the Dutch Republic in 1609, and in defusing the crisis over a disputed succession in Jülich-Cleves in 1614. He hoped to reinforce his position as a peace-broker by marriage alliances with both the Protestant and Catholic camps on the continent. The first stage in this plan was the marriage of his daughter, Elizabeth, to Frederick, the Protestant Elector Palatine, in 1613, and the following year he embarked on the quest for a marriage between his only surviving son, Charles, and the Infanta.

The pursuit of a Spanish match was to dominate James's foreign policy for the rest of his reign. He instructed Sir John Digby, the English Ambassador in Spain, to open negotiations, and James himself was on increasingly friendly terms with the Spanish Ambassador in London, the Count of Gondomar. Initially the negotiations proceeded quite well, if very slowly. Unfortunately for James, many of his subjects were profoundly hostile to the idea of a Spanish match, but what really wrecked the project was the outbreak of the Thirty Years' War in 1618, triggered by the revolt of the Protestant nobility of Bohemia against their Catholic King, the Habsburg Ferdinand of Styria. The following year James was placed in an extraordinarily difficult position when his son-in-law, the Elector Palatine, accepted the offer of the vacant throne of Bohemia without waiting for James's advice. This action was deeply insulting to Ferdinand, by now Holy Roman Emperor, and at the end of October 1620 the Catholic forces of the Habsburgs and the Duke of Bavaria routed Frederick's troops at the Battle of the White Mountain, drove him and Elizabeth out of Bohemia, and shortly afterwards occupied the Palatinate. Many in England regarded James's daughter and son-in-law as Protestant martyrs, and hoped that the King would intervene on their behalf. James pledged to restore the Palatinate, allowed a force of English volunteers to be assembled, and summoned Parliament to meet in January 1621.

However, while Parliament deliberated and then called for armed intervention on a scale well beyond what it was willing to finance, James continued to seek a peaceful solution. In the summer of 1621 he sent Digby to try to persuade the Emperor to withdraw from the Palatinate in return for Frederick's renunciation of the Bohemian throne, but neither party was prepared to agree to such terms. In the meantime, James took exception to the Commons' demands for a diversionary war against Spain and an immediate end to negotiations for a Spanish match, and informed the House that he was 'an old and experienced king needing no such lessons'. When the Commons drew up a protestation declaring that parliamentary free speech was 'the ancient and undoubted birthright and inheritance of the subjects of England', James tore the document out of the Commons' Journal and, possibly egged on by Gondomar, dissolved the Parliament.[24]

The dissolution of the 1621 Parliament was a major setback for James's foreign policy because it meant that henceforth he could not back up any threat with the reality of military force. Nevertheless, he continued to pursue a marriage alliance for his son with the Spanish

Infanta, hoping that the Spanish King might persuade his cousin the Emperor to grant concessions and restore the Palatinate. These hopes were idealistic, even naive, and they were soon overtaken by events. In February 1623 Prince Charles and Buckingham journeyed to Madrid in a last desperate bid to secure a Spanish match. But the visit was a fiasco: the Spanish dragged their feet over the negotiations and refused to let Charles meet the Infanta in person. Bitterly angry and disappointed, Charles and Buckingham returned home in October to popular rejoicing which demonstrated the depth of English hostility towards the Spanish match. Henceforth, the Prince and the Duke were determined to wage a war against Spain.

This was exactly what James had striven all along to prevent. He lamented that Charles was now 'strangely carried away with rash and youthful counsels, and followed the humour of Buckingham, who had he knew not how many devils within him since that journey'.[25] When Charles pressed him to use force against Spain, James allegedly burst into tears and protested: 'Do you want to commit me to war in my old age and make me break with Spain?'[26] This was indeed just what Charles and Buckingham wanted. They persuaded James to call another Parliament in February 1624, and mobilised a 'patriot' coalition in both Houses to push for war. James, however, remained anxious to avoid an open breach with Spain, and unlike many members of the Commons preferred to confine any military operations to securing the restoration of the Palatinate. Charles and Buckingham also pushed James to explore the possibility of a marriage alliance with France. With great reluctance, James agreed to sever the existing treaties with Spain in April 1624 and then to accept an Anglo-French marriage treaty the following November.

Yet even at this late stage James could not bring himself to abandon the Spanish negotiations completely. An expeditionary force led by the German mercenary Count Mansfeld was assembled to relieve the Palatinate, but James instructed them not to pass through any Spanish territories. The French resented this and retaliated by denying Mansfeld permission to land on their territory: as a result, Mansfeld was forced to land at Flushing, where a combination of disease, inadequate supplies and severe weather brought the expedition to a disastrous halt in January 1625. It was a sad conclusion to James's foreign policy, and an ominous warning of the difficulties that the early Stuart state encountered in pursuing an active military policy. Yet when James died in March 1625 England was still technically at peace, and he had succeeded in keeping out of – though not in resolving – the continental conflict. In retrospect his wish to avoid war had much to commend it in preventing undue strain on England's limited financial and military resources, and the experience of war during the opening years of Charles I's reign bore out James's wisdom in quoting the Latin motto 'dulce bellum inexpertis' ('war is only attractive to those who have not experienced it').[27]

In foreign policy, as in other areas, the accession of Charles I marked a watershed. Whereas James had unsuccessfully pursued peace and ended up on the brink of war, Charles unsuccessfully pursued war and by 1629–1630 ended up at peace. By 1625, Charles was the darling of the war party and when his sister Elizabeth learnt of his accession she allegedly declared: 'Now you may be sure all will go well in England.'[28] Charles immediately embarked on a two-pronged policy: to set the seal on an alliance with France, and to launch a naval expedition against Spain. It was utterly different from James's vision of international reconciliation, and it proved a disastrous failure. Within two years both of Charles's objectives lay in ruins.

Perhaps the central problem of Charles's foreign policy was his inability to secure the confidence and financial support of the political elite. This was reflected in the paradox that successive Parliaments called for war yet refused to grant adequate funds for it. Although the majority of members supported military action against the Habsburgs, in 1625 Charles's first Parliament refused to vote more than two subsidies (about £140,000) until they knew more about exactly what kind of war was envisaged. That autumn, Buckingham, as Lord High Admiral, led an expedition to Cadiz, but this bid to emulate Elizabethan naval exploits went seriously wrong. Poorly organised and inadequately supplied, the expedition failed to capture any of the Spanish fleet bringing bullion from the New World. Blame was heaped on Buckingham, although Charles maintained that the main problem was Parliament's refusal to grant adequate funding.

In the meantime, England's relations with France deteriorated badly. Charles had married Louis XIII's sister Henrietta Maria in May 1625, but the early years of their marriage were unhappy, and there were bitter recriminations over the implementation of the terms of the marriage treaty. Both England and France accused the other of infringing the terms of the agreement, and a strong personal antagonism grew up between Buckingham and Louis XIII's chief minister Richelieu. Under the terms of the treaty, England had agreed to loan France ships to assist in the suppression of a revolt by the Huguenot Duc de Soubise, but as the revolt spread to other Huguenot communities Charles refused to provide the ships so as not to be associated with wholesale attacks on French Protestantism. Only after prolonged controversy, which generated further bad feeling, were these loan ships eventually handed over. France and Spain meanwhile signed a peace in the spring of 1626, thus freeing

Louis's hand, and England and France slid towards war during the months that followed. England seized French ships allegedly carrying contraband to Spain; France retaliated by seizing the English wine fleet, and England declared war on France in January 1627. This was a complete disaster, for it was the worst possible scenario for early modern England to find herself at war with both France and Spain simultaneously.

Convinced that foreign affairs would never be successfully conducted while Buckingham remained so influential, the 1626 Parliament refused further supply until he was impeached. Charles retaliated by raising money without parliamentary consent, which was used to launch an expedition to relieve the Huguenots of La Rochelle in the summer of 1627. This proved another failure: the English troops were not equipped for a long siege, and when a direct assault was attempted it was found that the scaling-ladders they had brought were too short to surmount the walls of the citadel. It was another humiliating defeat for Buckingham.

Having exhausted the royal coffers, Charles had no option but to recall Parliament in 1628, and members bitterly condemned recent wartime policies, including the raising of a Forced Loan, the billeting of troops on civilians, and imprisonment without trial. In a corner, Charles was forced to accept the Petition of Right as the price for five subsidies which were vital for the continuance of the war. Even so, this sum was well below what was needed to furnish a really effective fighting force, and it is unlikely that many members of either House had much idea how expensive warfare had become by the 1620s, due to the 'military revolution' that took place in early modern Europe. Buckingham began preparations for another expedition to La Rochelle, but in August 1628 he was murdered at Portsmouth by a demobbed subaltern, John Felton. It was a crushing comment on Charles's failure to win support for his foreign policy that a former soldier should have murdered the Lord High Admiral and royal favourite.

The failure of the 1629 parliamentary session, and Charles's decision to embark on a period of personal rule, ensured that the war could not be continued much longer. The lack of parliamentary supply, and the intense unpopularity of non-parliamentary taxation, left Charles no option but to sue for peace. Agreement was soon reached with France, and the Treaty of Susa was signed on 24 April 1629. The treaty ended an essentially pointless war, and in restoring friendship between the two powers it carefully made no mention of the Huguenots. The negotiations with Spain took rather longer, and many committed Protestants in England lamented that the Treaty of Madrid (eventually signed on 5 November 1630) contained no guarantees for the restitution of the

Palatinate, despite Charles's pledge to the Elector Palatine that he would never conclude the Spanish war without such assurances. The treaty essentially restored the Treaty of London which James had signed in 1604. Interestingly, the Spanish envoy to England during these negotiations, the artist Peter Paul Rubens, later painted a brilliant ceiling for the Banqueting House in Whitehall that included a depiction of James I as peacemaker. It was deeply ironic that this ceiling was commissioned by Charles I, the monarch who had deliberately ended James's peaceful foreign policy, and was himself ultimately forced to withdraw from disastrous entanglement in continental war.

Ultimately, it is hard not to see James's pursuit of peace as preferable to Charles's pursuit of war. The worst that can be said of James is that he clung to his ideals after they had been overtaken by events, and that he was misled by others less principled than himself. But he understood the structural weaknesses that prevented the early Stuart state from pursuing an aggressive foreign policy, and eschewed war for practical as well as ethical reasons. Charles's policies starkly revealed England's military and financial limitations and fuelled mistrust between himself and many of his leading subjects. Two contemporary assessments sum up the contrasts between the foreign policies of James and Charles very neatly. Even one of James's most avowed enemies, Sir Anthony Weldon, conceded that James 'lived in peace, died in peace, and left all his kingdoms in a peaceable condition'.[29] By contrast, even one of Charles's most loyal supporters, Edward Hyde, Earl of Clarendon, admitted that 'in a time when all endeavours should have been used to have extinguished that war in which the kingdom was so unhappily engaged against Spain, a new war was as precipitately declared against France . . . the sad effects of [which] (if not instantly provided against) must inevitably destroy the kingdom'.[30]

Questions

1. How far were changing circumstances on the continent responsible for the failure of the foreign policies of both James VI and I and Charles I?
2. To what extent did Charles I's difficulties in foreign policy between 1625 and 1630 vindicate his father's attempts to preserve peace?

SOURCES

1. THE NATURE OF BUCKINGHAM

Source A: Sir John Eliot's speech to Parliament following the presentation of the impeachment charges against Buckingham, 10 May 1626.

First, I purpose [i.e. offer] unto your Lordships the inward character of the Duke's mind, which is full of collusion and deceit; I can express it no better than by the Beast, so called by the ancients Stellionatus;[31] a Beast so blurred, so spotted, so full of foul lines, that they knew not what to make of it; so do we find in this man's practice ... his design being against Rochelle and against the Religion ... He intercepts, consumes and exhausts the resources of the Crown ... and by emptying the veins the blood should run in he hath cast the body of the kingdom into an high consumption ... For his secret intentions and calumniations I wish this Parliament had not felt them, nor the other before. For his pride and flattery it is noted of Sejanus[32] that he did *Clientes suos Provinciis adornare* [adorn his clients with lands]. Doth not this man the like? Ask England, Scotland and Ireland and they will tell you. Sejanus' pride was so excessive, as Tacitus[33] saith.

Source B: Buckingham's response to the impeachment charges, 8 June 1626.

I have been raised to honour and fortunes in it [i.e. the state] (I freely confess) beyond my merit. What I have wanted [lacked] in sufficiency and experience for the service of it I have endeavoured to supply by care and industry [hard work], and could there be the least alienation hereafter of my heart from the service of the state for anything that hath passed, I should be the ungratefullest man living.

Source C: Lucy Hutchinson: *Memoirs of the Life of Colonel Hutchinson*. (Colonel Hutchinson was one of those who signed the death warrant of Charles I. He died in prison in 1664. His wife wrote his 'Memoirs' as a defence of his actions.)

[The people] began to entertain an universal hatred of the Duke of Buckingham, raised from a knight's fourth son to that pitch of glory and enjoying great possessions, acquired by the favour of the King upon no merit but that of his beauty ... The whole people were sadly grieved at these misgovernments [i.e. the foreign policy disasters of 1625–1627], and, loath to impute them to the King, cast all the odium [hatred] on the Duke of Buckingham, whom at length a discontented person stabbed, believing he did God and his country good service by it. All the kingdom ... rejoiced in the death of this Duke; but they found little cause, for after it the King still persisted in his design of enslaving them and found other ministers ready to serve his self-willed ambition.

Questions

1. Explain 'misgovernments', referred to in Source C. [2]
2. How reliable do you consider Source C for a historian researching the nature of the impact of the Duke of Buckingham? Your answer should refer to the origins and contents of this Source as well as other Sources in this collection and your own knowledge. [5]
*3. How useful is Source A for a historian researching the nature of the MPs who sat in the 1626 Parliament? [3]
4. Read Sources A and B. Referring to their tone and content, which of these speakers do you consider was the more effective in eliciting support from his audience? [8]
5. '[The people] began to entertain an universal hatred of the Duke of Buckingham.' Use these Sources and your own knowledge to explain why it is not surprising that the Duke was stabbed by a 'discontented person'. [7]

Worked answer

*3. *[The use of the word 'how' in the question demands a response which indicates ways in which the Source is useful and also ways in which it is not particularly useful.]*

It is useful in two main ways. First, since the speaker makes only oblique references to Buckingham's 'design' – 'Rochelle' and 'Religion' – and fails to explain his reference to how the Duke 'consumes and exhausts the resources of the Crown', it can be inferred that the political nation was already well informed about these matters. This in turn indicates to what extent Buckingham had become the source of a grievance by 1626. Second, Eliot's use of a Latin phrase and several classical references – 'Stellionatus', 'Sejanus' and 'Tacitus' – suggests that his audience was well versed in classical literature and thus provides a clue as to the nature of the education offered to the gentry at this time. On the other hand, the Source would be even more useful if we knew something of the reaction of the listeners to this oration. Without this information the historian can only assume that Eliot's references were understood.

SOURCES

2. THE FOREIGN POLICY OF JAMES VI AND I AND CHARLES I

Source D: A letter from the Duke of Buckingham to James VI and I, 3 March 1624.

I will forbear to tell them [i.e. MPs] that nothwithstanding of your cold you were able to speak with the King of Spain's instruments [i.e. representatives], though not with your own subjects. All I can say is, you march slowly towards your own safety [and that of] those that depend on you.

Source E: From a popular ballad of late 1623.

I would to God his Majesty
Of Spain were here awhile to see
The jollity of our English nation,
Then surely he would never hope
That either he or else the Pope
Could make here a Roman plantation.

Source F: James's response to the demand of the 1624 Parliament that the Spanish match be broken off.

He is an unhappy man, that shall advise a King to war; and it is an unhappy thing to seek that by blood, which may be had by peace ... To enter a war without sufficient means to support it, were to show my teeth, and do no more.

Source G: A letter from Zuane Pesaro, Venetian Ambassador in England, to the Doge and Senate of Venice, 4 July 1625.

His Majesty spoke to this effect, that the chief object for convoking [Parliament] was to receive assistance in the present great occasions for the recovery of the Palatinate ... He said that the preparations for war had been begun by the late King at the exhortation of Parliament; he was the King who was engaged and they were the ones who had committed him ... The members of Parliament ... contend that they have not committed the King, although they persuaded the abandonment of the negotiations with Spain ... The Parliament complains that the three subsidies granted to the late King were expended fruitlessly and ask to see the accounts.

Source H: A letter from Charles I to the Archbishop of Canterbury, George Abbot, 20 September 1626.

This war which grows full of danger was not entered upon rashly and without advice, but . . . by the counsel of both Houses of Parliament . . . Upon their persuasions and promises of all assistance and supply we readily undertook and effected and cannot now be left in that business but with the sin and shame of all men.

Source I: A letter from Sir Edward Conway, serving on the expedition to relieve La Rochelle, to Secretary Conway, 20 September 1627.

The army grows daily weaker, victuals waste, purses are empty, ammunition consumes, winter grows, their enemies increase in number and power, and they hear nothing from England.

Questions

1. (i)   Read Source D. Explain the phrase 'the King of Spain's instruments'. [2]
    (ii) Read Source E. Explain the phrase 'could make here a Roman plantation'. [2]
2. How far do Sources G–I bear out James's warning in Source F? [3]
3. What do these Sources reveal about the attitudes towards Spain of each of the following:
    (i)   James VI and I; [2]
    (ii) Charles I; [2]
    (iii) the Duke of Buckingham; [2]
    (iv) Parliament; [2]
    (v)   the English population generally? [2]
4. Using these Sources and your wider knowledge, how far were James's attempts to preserve peace unrealistic? [4]
*5. Using these Sources and your wider knowledge, consider who bears the greater responsibility for the failures of Charles I's foreign policy: the King or his Parliaments. [4]

Worked answer

*5. *[A good way to begin this answer would be to consider the various ways in which the King and Parliament were each responsible, and then assess which was more to blame.]*

These Sources suggest that Charles and his Parliaments should each bear some responsibility for the foreign policy failures.

Since 1621, successive Parliaments had been urging James and then Charles to take military action on the continent to recover the Palatinate. They desired, as a first step, negotiations for the Spanish match to be broken off, a demand which James only reluctantly agreed to, as Sources F and H make clear. King and Parliament seemed more at one upon Charles's accession to the throne because the new King strongly supported fighting a war against Spain, a consequence of the failure of his trip to Madrid in 1623. As such, he assumed that Parliament would grant him the necessary funds to do so. Indeed, given the enthusiastic support for war in the Parliaments of 1624 and 1625 – reflecting the popular mood as indicated by Source E – this was an understandable assumption.

However, Parliament was unwilling to give Charles a free hand to pursue whatever military campaigns he wished. It was reluctant to fund a war without having a say in its conduct and especially reluctant to support campaigns in which the hated favourite, Buckingham, played such a major role. Parliament blamed Buckingham for mishandling the situation and for involving England in what was widely regarded as an unnecessary war against France in 1627. Yet Charles blamed Parliament for not giving the necessary financial support for a war, despite the fact that it had come about in large part because of its 'exhortation' (Source G).

The fundamental problem lay in the growing mistrust between Charles and a significant proportion of his leading subjects, as represented in Parliament. Charles's failure to explain his policies adequately to Parliament, allied to his reluctance to discuss policy openly with MPs, meant that he was unable to build on the promising foundations of the 1624 Parliament. Here, as in so many other respects, the change of monarch was crucial, and the greater share of the responsibility for the failure of Charles's foreign policy should lie with the King himself.

5

CHARLES I

Rule with Parliaments, 1625–1629

BACKGROUND NARRATIVE

The opening years of Charles I's reign were troubled ones, marked by growing military and political crisis. At the time of his accession, England was in a state of undeclared war against Spain. In his first Parliament (June–August 1625) many members expressed growing concerns about the rise of anti-Calvinism in the Church, and they were reluctant to give much financial support for the war without further clarification about what military action was envisaged. In particular, they refused to vote the customs duties known as tonnage and poundage for more than a year. Traditionally, these had been granted to a new monarch for life, and after a year elapsed Charles continued to collect them anyway without parliamentary consent. In August Charles impatiently dissolved the Parliament, and the following month Buckingham embarked on the poorly funded and badly organised expedition to Cadiz that soon proved a disastrous failure.

Charles hoped that this fiasco would convince Parliament of the need to give generous supply, but when his second Parliament met (February–June 1626) he found that most members were more concerned to bring Buckingham to account. The King had to dissolve Parliament in order to prevent the Duke from being impeached, thereby losing the financial grants that Parliament had made conditional upon redress of grievances.

The failure of the 1626 Parliament forced Charles to turn to non-parliamentary forms of taxation, arguing that in such a wartime emergency his prerogative powers allowed him to do this. The benevolence (1626) yielded little money, but the Forced Loan (1627) was a considerable fiscal success. However, many people questioned the legality of such levies, and also that of some of Charles's other wartime policies, including the billeting of troops on civilians and the imprisonment of resisters without showing cause. The position was made much worse by the outbreak of war against France in January 1627 following disputes over the terms of the marriage agreement between Charles and Henrietta Maria, whom he had married in 1625. In the summer of 1627, Buckingham led an expedition to assist the Huguenot community of La Rochelle in defending their religious freedom against Louis XIII's forces, but this proved another military catastrophe.

Having exhausted the proceeds of the Forced Loan, financial need drove Charles to call another Parliament, which met in March 1628. Members devoted most of their time and energy to drafting the Petition of Right, which asserted the illegality of Charles's recent policies. Early in June, Charles reluctantly accepted the Petition in return for a grant of five subsidies. He was very angry when the Commons then presented a Remonstrance attacking Buckingham's conduct of the war, and promptly prorogued Parliament. Less than two months later, on 23 August, a demobbed soldier named John Felton assassinated Buckingham, an event that was greeted with such widespread rejoicing that his funeral had to be held at night.

Although many hoped that the Duke's death would improve matters, Charles persisted with unpopular policies, including the continued collection of tonnage and poundage, and the promotion of William Laud and his allies to senior bishoprics. The grievances came to a head when Parliament reassembled in January 1629. Instead of legitimating the collection of tonnage and poundage, as Charles had hoped, the Commons investigated why the Petition of Right had not been printed as a statute (an investigation that revealed Charles's underhand dealings). Furious, the King decided to dissolve Parliament. In the face of this, on 2 March, a group of members led by Denzil Holles and Benjamin Valentine restrained the Speaker while the Commons passed a Protestation denouncing innovation in religion, the spread of 'popery or Arminianism', and the payment or collection of tonnage and poundage (see Source D, below). On 10 March the King dissolved Parliament, blaming all the problems on a minority of 'ill-affected men' (see Source E, below), and ordered the arrest of nine members for their role in the events of 2 March. It would be eleven years before another Parliament was summoned.

ANALYSIS (1): WITH REFERENCE TO THE PERIOD 1625–1629, CONSIDER THE NOTION THAT CHARLES I WAS FUNDAMENTALLY UNSUITED TO THE TASK OF KINGSHIP.

At first sight, Charles I seemed very well suited to the task of kingship. His accession to the throne, in March 1625, was the smoothest and most peaceful since that of Henry VIII in 1509, and possibly since that of Henry V in 1413. He was a man in his mid-twenties and thus averted the dangers that contemporaries saw as the inevitable result of rule by a minor or a woman. He was a person of blameless moral character who quickly set about cleansing the Court of the promiscuity and corruption that had thrived there during his father's reign. Moreover, in the years immediately before James's death, and particularly in 1623–1625, his conversion to the cause of war against Spain had made him very popular in England. All that he lacked was a male heir, a deficiency that was put right in 1630 with the birth of the future Charles II. On the surface, Charles seemed to have all the makings of an outstanding monarch.

But appearances can be deceptive, for some of Charles's other characteristics left him much less equipped to rule the Stuart monarchies. In a personal monarchy, such as England, Scotland and Ireland were in this period, the personality, beliefs and political style of the monarch had a direct impact on the conduct of government and the nature of political life. Such a system was inevitably vulnerable whenever there was a change of monarch, and contemporaries immediately noticed that Charles was a very different character from his father. In place of James's earthy gregariousness and political flexibility, Charles was much more aloof and much less willing to compromise on his principles. He was coolly dignified in manner, with a passion for order and formality, and a self-righteous belief in his own rectitude. He wished always to define issues and reacted very badly to the slightest hint of disloyalty or disagreement.

Had these been purely personal characteristics they might not have posed much of a problem. But inevitably they also had a negative effect on Charles's political behaviour. The conduct of government in early modern England ultimately rested on three institutions which G. R. Elton called the 'points of contact': Parliament, the Privy Council and the Court.[1] These acted as vital channels through which the monarch and the leading subjects could exchange information and opinions. However, between 1625 and 1629 it became increasingly clear that Charles's personality was not ideally suited to ensuring the smooth running of any of them.

Although Charles expressed in theory a willingness to work with Parliaments, in practice his treatment of them was unfortunate in several ways. He was a man of few words – in marked contrast to his father – and because of his stutter he disliked speaking in public. In his opening speech to his first Parliament, he informed members that it did not 'stand with my nature to spend much time in words'.[2] This trait made it much harder for members of the Lords and Commons to get to know Charles, whereas they had always appreciated where they stood with James, even if they disagreed with him. They also found that Charles was assertive and aggressive by his actions rather than his words. He tended to blame his problems with Parliaments on a minority of 'ill-affected' members who led the loyal majority astray (see Source E, below). Yet this view soon proved self-fulfilling, for the sterner the measures he took against his opponents, such as appointing leading critics as sheriffs to exclude them from the 1626 Parliament, the more moderate members he alienated. He became increasingly impatient with Parliaments and barely a year after his accession was exploring means to make non-parliamentary government financially viable, notably the benevolence and the Forced Loan. Many members came to fear for the future of Parliaments, such as Sir Benjamin Rudyerd who reportedly warned in March 1628 that 'this is the crisis of parliaments; by this we shall know whether parliaments will live or die'.[3] Some of Charles's actions also made many members mistrust him: for example, although he eventually assented to the Petition of Right in June 1628, he later secretly instructed the royal printer to erase its statute number, thereby casting doubt upon its status as a statute and making it much more difficult for anyone to challenge the King's subsequent actions by citing the Petition in the courts.[4] Charles clearly believed that such methods were legitimate ways of defending his powers against parliamentary encroachment, but to many of his subjects they appeared duplicitous and disturbing.

Another reason for growing mistrust of Charles, both within Parliament and more widely, was his choice of advisers. Charles remained deeply loyal to Buckingham even though many blamed the Duke for disastrously mishandling England's wars against France and Spain between 1625 and 1628. The King refused to listen to those who denounced Buckingham, and in June 1626 dissolved Parliament when it threatened to impeach the Duke. Instead, the Privy Council became dominated by those sympathetic to Buckingham, and during these years the Duke acquired a virtual stranglehold on the distribution of patronage. Those Privy Councillors who criticised policies like the Forced Loan (such as the Earl of Pembroke and Viscount Saye) were either marginalised or replaced by 'new counsels' more sympathetic to Charles and Buckingham.[5] As a result, the Privy Council became much less effective as a channel of communication through which Charles could gauge opinion in the nation as a whole.

Much the same was true of the royal Court. Charles's energetic reforms of the Court, and their consequences, will be discussed more fully in Chapter 6. Here we should note that from the beginning of his reign Charles effectively debarred from the Court anyone who criticised royal policies, thus making it much less effective as a 'point of contact' than the Jacobean Court, which despite its undeniable seediness and corruption did at least permit a range of political opinions to be heard.

In performing the key role of Supreme Governor of the Church, Charles proved similarly unable to win the confidence of a majority of his subjects. During these early years many were increasingly disturbed by his strong support for those clergy often branded 'Arminians'. One in particular, Richard Montagu, had caused intense controversy at the end of James I's reign by playing down the doctrinal differences between the Churches of England and Rome. Charles's decisions to appoint Montagu a royal chaplain (July 1625) and then Bishop of Chichester (July 1628) were remarkable slaps in the face for many members of Parliament. The King's promotion of another leading 'Arminian', William Laud, to the bishopric of London (July 1628), and Buckingham's clear support of the 'Arminians' at the York House Conference in February 1626 were further indications of the same trend. Such actions could scarcely have been more calculated to upset the delicate balance of the Jacobean Church: they profoundly alarmed committed Protestants and turned fear of religious innovation into a standing political issue in a way that it had never been under James.

These problems were compounded by the fact that Charles reacted very badly to criticism and soon developed an almost obsessive sensitivity to any sign of disloyalty or subversion. Unable to accept that alternative opinions might be as sincerely held as his own, he found it difficult to engage in dialogue and found the rough and tumble of political life very uncongenial. This made it very hard to express opposition to royal policies through legitimate channels, or to persuade the King to accept advice, and when he did listen to counsel, it was often in a selective and idiosyncratic manner.[6] As one of Charles's Secretaries of State, Sir John

Coke, later observed: 'Kings cannot be served against their will.'[7] Indeed, there are signs that Charles was not really a political animal at all and that his main interests lay elsewhere: in that sense also he was not temperamentally well suited to kingship. One glimpse of Charles in late 1631 neatly sums this up. One afternoon, Secretary Dorchester needed to confer urgently with the King about the possibility of concluding an alliance with Sweden. Clutching vital diplomatic correspondence, he eventually came upon Charles in the picture gallery at Whitehall. There he found the King 'seriously employed' in 'the midst of his antique pictures . . . placing and removing his emperors' heads and putting them in right order'. Only when that task was finished was Charles prepared to turn his mind towards pressing matters of contemporary foreign policy.[8] It was a telling reflection on a King who was more interested in the visual arts than in the arts of government.

Questions

1. Assess the strengths and weaknesses of Charles I as a monarch during the early years of his reign.
2. A 'breakdown in communication' or a 'fundamental ideological divide': which of these better explains the growing tension between Charles I and his opponents during the later 1620s?

ANALYSIS (2): FOR WHAT REASONS DID CHARLES I DECIDE TO RULE WITHOUT PARLIAMENTS FROM 1629?

Historians remain divided over whether, when Charles dissolved Parliament in March 1629, he intended to rule without Parliaments for the foreseeable future. It is possible that initially he wished to keep his options open, and that it was only by the early 1630s that he became determined not to face another Parliament except in an absolute emergency.[9] What we can be sure of is that by March 1629 his patience with Parliaments, and his willingness to work with them, had reached breaking point. This was a direct consequence of his experiences of Parliaments since his accession. Ironically, Charles had initially felt very positively about Parliaments. He met with three different Parliaments during the first five years of his reign (every year from 1625 to 1629 except 1627), a rate well above the average for the sixteenth and seventeenth centuries as a whole. In the years immediately before his accession, Charles had been very popular with many members of Parliament, and Sir Benjamin Rudyerd praised him as 'a prince bred up in Parliaments'.[10] However, by

1629 he had become deeply disillusioned with Parliaments and regarded them as obstacles to smooth and effective government. What had gone wrong?

One key element in Charles's gradual disenchantment with Parliaments was his frustration with their reluctance to grant him the financial support that he required. At the beginning of his reign, instead of following the customary practice of granting the new monarch tonnage and poundage for life, the Commons voted it for only one year pending a full-scale review of royal revenues. However, the Parliament was dissolved before this review was completed, and when Charles proceeded to collect tonnage and poundage after the first year had elapsed the issue became a standing grievance between him and Parliament. In 1626 the Commons withheld supply while they attempted to impeach Buckingham, and in 1628 they voted only five subsidies after securing the King's consent to the Petition of Right. To Charles it seemed that Parliament was urging him to engage in war on the continent and then refusing to give him adequate means to fund it. In such circumstances, he thought it reasonable to use the royal prerogative to levy non-parliamentary taxation in the form of the benevolence and the Forced Loan.

One of Parliament's principal reasons for withholding supply was its intense hostility towards Buckingham and its lack of confidence in his leadership. Members were very unwilling to throw good money after bad, especially in view of the Duke's disastrous expeditions to Cadiz in 1625 and La Rochelle in 1627. Charles, on the other hand, believed that if Parliament would only grant sufficient financial support, England's war effort would stand a much better chance of success. He remained deeply loyal to Buckingham and bitterly resented Parliament's attempt to impeach the Duke in 1626, and their Remonstrance against his conduct of the war in 1628. Charles never forgave Sir John Eliot for likening Buckingham to Sejanus, the hated adviser to the tyrannical Emperor Tiberius (see Chapter 4, Source A).[11] The King was convinced that Parliament's relentless attacks on Buckingham played a significant part in encouraging John Felton to assassinate him in August 1628, and the Duke's murder, far from improving relations between the King and Parliament, thus significantly worsened them.

Parliament's attempts to dislodge Buckingham appeared to Charles to be part of a more general encroachment upon royal powers. He was appalled at the Houses' refusal to support what he regarded as essential wartime measures, such as the raising of taxation by authority of the royal prerogative, the billeting of troops on civilians, and the imprisonment of those who were obstructive. Parliament's disquiet culminated in the

Petition of Right in 1628, which cited Magna Carta and a series of medieval statutes to spell out the legal safeguards against the abuse of royal powers. To Charles it seemed that Parliament was taking too much upon itself and seeking to police powers that were by definition discretionary. He only accepted the Petition with great reluctance, and later tried to cast doubt on its status as a statute.[12] Charles similarly resented the Protestation which the Commons passed on 2 March 1629, denouncing those who brought in 'innovation of religion', and those who encouraged or contributed to the payment of tonnage and poundage (see Source D, below). Once again, to Charles this looked like the deliberate obstructiveness of a group of trouble-makers, and he ordered the arrest of nine members of the Commons shortly afterwards.

The Protestation's inclusion of religion brings us to another major reason for Charles's disillusionment with Parliament, namely many members' fear of 'popery' and 'Arminianism', and their opposition to the 'ceremonialist' practices in the Church which he encouraged. Charles regarded the Commons' attack on Richard Montagu in 1625 as vindictive and misguided, and he feared that behind it lay a Puritan campaign against anyone within the Church who was perceived as at all sympathetic towards Rome. In 1629 the Commons' concerns prompted it to appoint a committee to consider the state of the Church. This committee proposed a series of resolutions, condemning the 'subtle and pernicious spreading of the Arminian faction' and requesting that the King 'be graciously pleased to confer bishoprics, and other ecclesiastical preferments, with the advice of his Privy Council, upon learned, pious and orthodox men'.[13] Charles regarded this as an infringement of his right to make clerical appointments under the royal supremacy, and it reinforced his hostility towards those of a Puritan persuasion. Throughout the later 1620s he found the so-called 'Arminians' consistently more supportive of royal policies, as, for example, in Sibthorpe's sermon in defence of the Forced Loan (see Source G, below) than those at the opposite end of the religious spectrum (see Source J, below).

This perception in turn reinforced Charles's belief that the parliamentary opposition to him formed an ideologically coherent conspiracy. He saw a direct link between Puritanism and a populist assault upon the royal prerogative, and he believed that a significant minority of members were determined to use Parliament to promote such a campaign. He was not alone in this view. In 1626 an anonymous author described the parliamentary attack on Buckingham as the work of popular spirits in the Commons who sought 'the debasing of this free monarchy'. The author cited Puritans and sectaries as prominent among the malcontents likely to support this conspiracy.[14] The problem was that once Charles had become convinced of the reality of a conspiracy, he then read every sign of parliamentary opposition as a manifestation of it. However, the very measures that he took to counteract it only appeared to confirm the worst fears of his parliamentary critics. The central problem of the years 1625–1629 was thus a gradual breakdown of trust between the King and his Parliaments. Once mutual trust had become eroded, the fears of each side became self-fulfilling and generated a political atmosphere in which each was paranoid about possible conspiracies by the other. This produced a vicious circle that culminated in the breach of 1629.

It was an ironic outcome in two particular ways. First, it is probable that Charles's very positive early experiences of Parliament, especially in 1624, were counter-productive in that they lulled him into a false sense of security and convinced him that Parliaments were straightforward to manage. With great prescience, James warned Charles in 1624 that he 'would live to have his bellyful of Parliaments'.[15] When Charles was then faced, after 1625, with growing parliamentary opposition, his instinctive reaction was a kind of self-righteous bewilderment allied to a conviction that the problems must be the work of an 'ill-affected' minority. The very fact that he had been so warmly fêted by Parliament immediately before his accession left him poorly prepared to handle the difficult wartime Parliaments of 1625–1629.

The second irony is that the very frequency of Parliaments during the early years of Charles's reign may have helped to undermine political stability. The fact that Parliament met in four of Charles's first five years as King (as opposed, for example, to nine of James's twenty-two years on the throne, or fifteen of Elizabeth's forty-five) meant that a higher proportion of members than usual sat in successive Parliaments.[16] During the later 1620s, there was less time in between parliamentary sessions for tempers to cool, and as a result there was much greater continuity of personnel and of the issues that were debated than in the two preceding reigns. As a result, the relationships between the monarch and members of Parliament became more important than ever, and when trust broke down between them Charles ultimately saw no alternative to ruling without Parliaments. By 1629, his experience of Parliaments since his accession had convinced him that on balance their benefits were not worth the political hassle that they involved. He had come to a view that he could attain more of his goals, and achieve greater political stability, if he embarked on a period of rule without Parliaments.

Questions

1. How far were Charles I's fears about Parliaments self-fulfilling prophecies?

2. To what extent did members of the Houses of Parliament believe that the King was encroaching on their rights and privileges in the years 1625–1629, and was such a belief justified?

SOURCES

1. THE CONTEXT OF THE DISSOLUTION OF PARLIAMENT IN 1629

Source A: From a declaration to Parliament drafted by Charles and his advisers early in May 1628 but never published.

Some of the members of that house [of Commons] ... have, under the specious show of redeeming the liberty of the subject, endeavoured to destroy our just power of sovereignty ... They have long debated and, without our privity [i.e. being consulted], concluded upon a declaration of the just liberty of the subject [the Petition of Right, which] ... would so undermine our sovereignty and regal power that we should thereby be deprived of means to govern and protect our people ... [and it] would soon dissolve the very frame and foundations of a monarchy.

Source B: From the Petition of Right, to which Charles I assented on 7 June 1628.

[The Lords and Commons] humbly pray your Most Excellent Majesty that no man hereafter be compelled to make or yield any gift, loan, benevolence, tax, or such like charge, without common consent by Act of Parliament; ... and that no freeman ... be imprisoned or detained [without cause shown]; and that your Majesty will be pleased to remove the ... soldiers and mariners [billeted on civilians], and that your people may not be so burdened in time to come; and that the ... commissions for proceeding by martial law may be revoked and annulled ... All which they most humbly pray your Most Excellent Majesty, as their rights and liberties according to the laws and statutes of this realm.

Source C: Charles I's first answer to the Petition of Right, 2 June 1628.

The King willeth that right be done according to the laws and customs of the realm; and that the statutes be put in due execution, that his subjects may have no cause to complain of any wrong or oppressions, contrary to their just rights and liberties, to the preservation whereof he holds himself as well obliged as of his prerogative.

Source D: From the Protestation of the House of Commons, 2 March 1629.

1. Whosoever shall bring in innovation of religion, or . . . seem to extend or introduce popery or Arminianism, . . . shall be reputed a capital enemy to this kingdom and commonwealth.

2. Whosoever shall counsel or advise the taking and levying of the subsidies of tonnage and poundage, not being granted by Parliament . . . shall be likewise reputed an innovator in the government, and a capital enemy to the kingdom and commonwealth.

3. If any merchant or person whatsoever shall voluntarily yield, or pay the said subsidies of tonnage and poundage, not being granted by Parliament, he shall likewise be reputed a betrayer of the liberties of England, and an enemy to the same.

Source E: From the King's Declaration showing the causes of the late dissolution, 10 March 1629.

No sooner therefore was the Parliament set down [in January 1629] but . . . ill-affected men began to sow and disperse their jealousies . . . The sincerer and better part of the House [of Commons] was overborne by the practices and clamours of the other, who, careless of their duties, and taking advantage of the times and our necessities, have enforced us to break off this meeting.

Questions

1. (i) Read Source A. Why might Charles have feared that some members of the Commons 'endeavoured to destroy our just power of sovereignty'? [2]
   (ii) Read Source D. Comment on the phrase 'to extend or introduce popery or Arminianism'. [2]

2. What do Sources A and E reveal about Charles's view of Parliament? [5]

3. Do Sources B and D offer any evidence either to support or to refute Charles's claims in Sources A and E? [6]

*4. Why might Parliament have been dissatisfied with Charles's first answer to the Petition of Right, given in Source C? [3]

5. With reference to these Sources and your own knowledge, who was more to blame for the King's decision to rule without Parliament in 1629: Charles I or Parliament? [7]

Worked answer

*4. *[Examine closely the content and wording of Charles's first answer, and consider how it fell short of what Parliament had hoped for.]*

Members found Charles's answer evasive and non-committal. He did not respond to the Petition as such, or even address it, but simply confirmed the existing laws. By inserting a phrase saving his prerogative, he also rendered the Petition useless because such a get-out clause could be used to mean whatever Charles wanted it to mean. This answer would have allowed Charles to continue to behave as though nothing had changed, and the Commons not surprisingly refused to proceed with granting supply until the King unconditionally assented to the Petition of Right as it stood.

SOURCES

2. THE FORCED LOAN

Source F: From the King's Proclamation of 7 October 1626.

We had resolved, for the necessary defence of our honour, our religion, and kingdoms, to require the aid of our loving subjects in that way of loan ... No other possible and present course [is] to be taken, nor this to be avoided, if we as King shall maintain the cause and party of religion, preserve our own honour, defend our people, secure our kingdoms and support our allies ... Nevertheless, we are resolved ... that this course, which at this time is thus inforced upon us by that necessity, ... shall not in any wise be drawn into example, nor made a precedent for after times.

Source G: From Robert Sibthorpe's sermon *Apostolike Obedience* (1627).

If a prince impose an immoderate, yea an unjust tax, yet the subject may not thereupon withdraw his obedience and duty; nay he is bound in conscience to submit, as under the scourge for his sin.

Source H: From *The Acts of the Privy Council* for February 1627.

George Catesbye of [blank] in the county of Northampton ... [declared] His Majesty's intention in this way of the loan was no warrant to the subject to trust to, for though the King in one place says it shall not be made a precedent, yet ... the proclamation ... was no security to the subject ... proclamations are alterable at the King's pleasure, therefore they do not bind ... Hereupon the [Privy Council] censured him for this cause to be committed to the Marshalsea [a prison at Southwark].

Source I: From an anonymous manuscript pamphlet, possibly by the Earl of Lincoln, entitled 'To all English Freeholders from a Well-Wisher of Theirs', and dated 24 January 1627.

Beware and consider what you do concerning these subsidies and loans which are now demanded of you, lest you give away not only your money but your liberty and property in your own goods ... If this course be not withstood, but take effect, we shall be ourselves the instruments of our own slavery and the loss of the privilege which we have hitherto enjoyed, that our goods cannot be taken from us without consent of Parliament.

Source J: From a manuscript treatise by the Canterbury alderman Thomas Scott.

The puritan's conscience consists (in some cases) in disobedience ... In general all judicious puritans hold that it is against conscience to yield obedience to tyrannical and lawless commands as of duty ... Yea, gracious subjects ought of duty in their places to discountenance and dishearten graceless tyrants.

Questions

1. Read Source J. Comment on the significance of the phrases 'tyrannical and lawless commands' and 'graceless tyrants'. [2]
2. Read Source F, and the attack on it reported in Source H. Which do you find more convincing, and why? [5]
3. Source G is an extract from a sermon delivered by an 'Arminian' cleric. Comment on the significance and implications of this. [5]
4. With reference to these Sources and your own knowledge, how well grounded were the warnings given in Sources I and J? [6]
*5. With reference to these Sources and your own knowledge, in what ways did the Forced Loan damage relations between King and Parliament in the later 1620s? [7]

Worked answer

*5. *[It is important here to explore and analyse the range of politically damaging implications of the Loan.]*

The Forced Loan contributed significantly to the breakdown of trust between the King and Parliament. It revealed Charles's willingness to use his prerogative powers to levy taxation on his own authority, without Parliament's consent. It thus demonstrated his growing impatience with Parliaments and his readiness to govern without them. The very fact that the Loan was such a financial success (over £240,000 of the £300,000 that Charles demanded was raised within a year) reinforced members' fears for the future of Parliament as an institution. As Sir Benjamin Rudyerd put it in March 1628, 'this is the crisis of parliaments; by this we shall know whether parliaments will live or die'. Parliament's survival, and that of the liberties which it safeguarded, appeared to be in jeopardy, a point strongly made in Source J. Such anxieties were deepened by the fact that despite the King's reassurances (in Source F), there was no guarantee that the Loan would not be used as a precedent, to be repeated regularly in the future (this view is forcefully expressed in Source I).

Also destabilising was the fact that the Loan proved very divisive. In some ways it might have been less problematic had it been either unanimously supported or unanimously resisted. But the fact that the Loan inspired strong and conflicting views both for and against it seriously eroded harmony between Crown and Parliament. These divisions were made worse by the fact that they corresponded quite closely with the growing religious discords of these years. The so-called 'Arminians' generally defended the Loan, and strongly advocated its payment, as Source G illustrates. By contrast, Source J reveals that the 'puritans' recognised an equally strong duty to refuse payment. These attitudes only appeared to confirm the worst fears that each side harboured of the other, and this divisiveness further disrupted the body politic.

Although a fiscal success, the Loan was thus politically very damaging, and it played a large part in making the Parliament of 1628–1629 so troubled. It loomed large in the debates on the Petition of Right, and the Petition explicitly denied the legality of such loans when raised without Parliament's consent. The Loan polarised opinion and left a legacy of grievance and mistrust that infected the Parliament of 1628–1629, thereby directly contributing to the King's decision to rule without Parliaments.

6

CHARLES I

Rule without Parliaments, 1629–1640

BACKGROUND NARRATIVE

Shortly after he dissolved Parliament in March 1629, Charles I issued a proclamation declaring that he would not recall Parliament until 'our people shall see more clearly into our intents and actions'.[1] His decision to rule without Parliaments for the foreseeable future may not have hardened into a firm resolve until about 1632; but in the meantime he realised that his involvement in continental warfare could not continue without parliamentary supply. He therefore signed the Treaty of Susa (14 April 1629) with France and then the Treaty of Madrid (5 November 1630) with Spain.

In order to balance his budget, Charles revived a number of financial levies that had fallen into disuse. In 1630 he appointed a commission to fine those who owned freehold land yielding £40 a year, but who had ignored the precedents requiring them to present themselves to the King to be knighted. This practice, known as 'distraint of knighthood', raised a total of nearly £175,000 by 1640. From 1634, Charles revived ancient forest courts to fine those who had inadvertently encroached on the medieval boundaries of royal forests, and over the next six years these forest fines yielded about £40,000. By far the most controversial of these financial expedients was Ship Money. From the reign of Edward III, this had occasionally been levied on coastal towns in national emergencies to equip a fleet to defend the realm. Charles raised it annually between 1634 and 1639, and from 1635 extended it to the whole nation. The legality of raising Ship Money in peacetime, and throughout England, proved highly contentious, yet over 90 per cent of the assessments were paid. These financial expedients were very successful, and by 1637 Charles's annual revenue exceeded £1 million: this was 50 per cent higher than in 1625, and in real terms double James I's income in 1603.

As a result, provided that he avoided a major military conflict, Charles was financially independent of Parliament, and this enabled him to set about reforming the Court, the institutions of central and local government, and the Church. Although these policies were far from universally popular, little overt hostility was expressed and outwardly for much of the 1630s there was an air of orderly calm.

The personal rule might well have lasted longer had it not been for Charles's introduction of a new Prayer Book in Scotland in 1637 which precipitated a rebellion in his northern kingdom. Rather than grant concessions, Charles embarked on two disastrous military campaigns against the Scots which brought him to the verge of bankruptcy and forced him to summon two Parliaments in 1640. It was thus one of Charles's own reforming initiatives that was ultimately responsible for bringing his period of rule without Parliaments to a dramatic end.

ANALYSIS (1): A PERIOD OF 'PERSONAL RULE' OR 'ELEVEN YEARS' TYRANNY': WHICH OF THESE IS THE BETTER DESCRIPTION OF CAROLINE GOVERNMENT IN ENGLAND DURING THE 1630s?

The terms 'personal rule' and 'eleven years' tyranny' both reflect a particular historiographical interpretation of Charles I's regime during the 1630s. The Whig historians, epitomised by S. R. Gardiner, lent support to the phrase 'eleven years' tyranny' by presenting this period as one of authoritarian government in which the King showed little respect for property, liberty or the rule of law.[2] Against this, more recent scholars, most notably Kevin Sharpe, have preferred the more neutral term 'personal rule' as a straightforwardly factual description of years in which the King did not call Parliament and ruled entirely through the institutions of personal government, such as the Privy Council. Sharpe in particular has also argued that this was a period of positive reform, vigorously pursued by a monarch with a genuine vision of an orderly commonwealth.[3] It is important not only to examine each of these interpretations in turn, but to realise that both views resemble how some of Charles's subjects saw things at the time. The fundamental problem with Caroline government in the 1630s was thus not that it provoked unanimous hostility, but rather that it divided the nation in a manner which ultimately proved even more dangerous.

According to the 'eleven years' tyranny' interpretation, during the absence of Parliaments Charles ruled in certain ways that violated his subjects' liberties and property. One major example of this was his use of prerogative powers to raise revenue without parliamentary consent. Although medieval precedents existed for knighthood fines, forest fines and even for Ship Money, Charles was nevertheless pushing his powers to their furthest limit and using them so widely and energetically that some of his subjects began to question their legality. Ship Money posed a particular problem in that while it was generally accepted that the monarch could raise it in a national emergency (such as time of war or imminent invasion), its legality during peacetime was much less clear.

In 1637 John Hampden refused to pay Ship Money, asserting the principle of no taxation without parliamentary consent. In the test case which followed, a minority of judges found for Hampden, including Sir Richard Hutton, who asserted that 'the people of England are subjects, not slaves; freemen not villeins; and are not to be taxed . . . at will, but according to the laws of this kingdom'.[4] The judges were not alone in being unable to agree: for example, some Kentish gentry accepted the legality of Ship Money, but others asserted that 'the King had not an absolute power . . . [and] hath no prerogative but that which the law of the land doth give and allow'.[5] At the heart of the controversy lay two intractable questions. First, how far was the King abusing his prerogative powers by using them in inappropriate circumstances? And second, was all property ultimately derived from the Crown and therefore revocable by it, or did the common law protect property owners and ensure that public revenues could only be raised with their consent? These questions divided Charles's subjects and there were no ready answers to them.

The impression of royal high-handedness was increased by the lack of consultation over official policies, and by the savage penalties imposed on some of those who criticised them. The Privy Council was the principal organ of central government, and in the absence of Parliaments it handled an even greater volume and range of business than usual. In all, it met over 1,000 times between March 1629 and April 1640. Yet Charles increasingly relied on an inner circle of advisers, including William Laud, Sir Thomas Wentworth, Secretary Windebank and Lord Treasurer Weston, and those who registered any dissent from the King's policies found themselves marginalised or excluded. The same was largely true of Charles's Court, which was much more self-contained and detached from the outside world than his father's. All of this made it very difficult for critics of the regime to voice their opposition legitimately and in ways that the King would accept. Among the most dramatic episodes of the 1630s were the exemplary punishments (including heavy fines and ear-cropping) meted out to those who openly criticised official policies, especially in the Church, such as Alexander Leighton, William Prynne, Henry Burton and John Bastwick. These were professional men of high social status and there was widespread consternation that they were punished in this way. It was during this period that Star Chamber acquired the dark reputation for brutal penalties which ultimately led to its abolition in 1641.

Although high profile, these Puritan 'martyrs' were not numerous, and Charles's government (like other early modern European regimes) lacked either the will or the resources to implement anything resembling a reign of terror. Some contemporaries did, however, regard Charles's drive for order and uniformity as intrusive. A series of proclamations ordered gentry to reside in their counties rather than in London; others restricted access to the Court for those wishing to be touched for the 'King's Evil' (scrofula). In 1631 Charles issued a new Book of Orders urging Justices of the Peace to be more vigorous in enforcing statutes and requiring them to report back to the Privy Council about a wide range of local matters. He also made concerted efforts to improve the effectiveness of county militias, but this was widely perceived as another example of central interference. Thus, although little in Charles's policies was unambiguously illegal, there was much that could legitimately be seen as authoritarian. It has also been argued that Charles's regime was so fearful of public criticism that it imposed widespread censorship and that there were significant restrictions on freedom of expression in print during the 1630s.[6] Once all this is combined with a Whiggish belief that any prolonged period of rule without Parliaments was unnatural and inherently despotic, it is not difficult to see how the term 'eleven years' tyranny' gained currency.

On the other hand, 'revisionist' historians, especially Kevin Sharpe, have argued that scholars have for too long viewed the 1630s through the eyes of Charles's opponents and have neglected the positive aspects of these years. He suggests instead that Charles pursued a positive programme of reform, guided by a coherent vision of Church and state, that opposition to his policies has been exaggerated, and that these were years of stability and calm.

At the heart of Charles's regime lay two institutions: the Court and the Privy Council. In the absence of Parliaments, the Council became Charles's principal instrument for implementing reform. He streamlined its procedures and record-keeping to ensure that it could handle an ever-growing volume and range of business promptly and efficiently. Charles attended Privy Council meetings far more assiduously than James had done and prepared very carefully for them. He showed a similar desire to regulate the royal Court and to transform his father's promiscuous and disorganised Court into a model of order, formality and ceremonial. Meticulously detailed books of Household Ordinances – with each page individually autographed by Charles – laid down with minute precision every aspect of the workings of the Court. An effective campaign was launched to reduce pilfering and wastage. There was a strict hierarchy governing which officials had access to which parts of the palace of Whitehall, and in 1636–1637 Charles had all the locks changed and issued fastidious instructions concerning who received which new keys. Everywhere there was order, dignity and decorum, epitomised by the King's revival of the annual ceremonies of the Order of the Garter at Windsor Castle.

These reforms went together with some remarkable cultural achievements. The King instructed Inigo Jones's pupil John Webb to design a magnificent new baroque palace, comparable with the great royal palaces of Spain or France, to replace the old palace of Whitehall. Charles was a great patron of the arts: he bought many paintings and sculptures from the continent, and painters such as Van Dyck and Rubens did some of their finest work in response to royal commissions. Many of their paintings portrayed the power of the monarch to impose order on chaos, a theme that was also evident in the Court masques performed regularly throughout the personal rule. Yet there was something closed and unreal about the Caroline Court. Many of Charles's subjects found his cultural tastes dangerously tainted by continental Catholicism and royal absolutism. There was also concern at the distancing of the Court from the nation at large, and the difficulty that ordinary people found in getting anywhere near Charles, not least those hoping to be touched for the 'King's Evil'.

In a sense, the Court provided a model for the orderliness and uniformity that Charles hoped to extend to the whole nation. He wanted the nobility and gentry to discharge their responsibilities as local governors more effectively. The Book of Orders and the attempts to create an 'exact militia' in each county were parts of this effort, as were Charles's concerted measures to get the nobility and gentry to live in their counties rather than in London. Perhaps the most dramatic attempts to introduce nationwide reforms were in the Church, a subject that will be analysed more fully below. The 'revisionists' have also asserted that official efforts to control the printing press during the 1630s were much more limited than has often been supposed, and that the regime lacked both the machinery and the will to impose anything resembling full-scale censorship.[7] All in all, in arguing that these years saw sustained and vigorous reform, driven by a monarch with a very clear idea of how he wished to remodel his realm, the 'revisionist' historians have certainly helped us to appreciate how the period looked through the eyes of Charles and his closest advisers.

This historiographical debate corresponds closely to differing contemporary views of these years. Whig historians could point to evidence of intensely felt grievances, such as the extraordinary outburst of hostility against recent royal policies voiced when Parliament reassembled in 1640. By contrast, Clarendon wrote that during the 1630s England 'enjoyed the greatest calm and the fullest measure of felicity that any people in any age for so long time together have been blessed with'.[8] The crucial problem was not that Charles's policies were universally unpopular, but that they were deeply divisive. The contrasting interpretations summed up by the phrases 'eleven years' tyranny' and 'the personal rule' can be traced back to the profound differences of perception that developed within England at the time.

A further problem concerns the definition of tyranny. John Morrill has written that 'the concept of tyranny was one widely used and understood and yet fuzzily defined in the early seventeenth century'.[9] There was no agreed definition of what constituted tyranny. It was, however, widely believed that certain actions could be lawful yet also tyrannical. Sir John Eliot wrote that the difference between a lawful king and a tyrant was that a true king 'will not do what he may'. Thus, as R. W. K. Hinton argued, when 'Charles I did only what the law allowed, this does not mean that he acted correctly'.[10] In the early seventeenth century many believed that the misuse of agreed royal powers – such as using them in inappropriate circumstances, or for personal rather than national benefit – constituted tyranny. It was thus no answer to Charles's critics to claim that he behaved legally or according to precedent, for such actions could still be regarded as tyrannical.

Of the two labels, 'the personal rule' is clearly the more neutral: it does not necessarily imply a positive view of Charles I and his policies, whereas 'the eleven years' tyranny' necessarily implies a negative one. In that sense, 'the personal rule' has the advantage of being a less loaded term. It also helpfully captures the fact that Charles's personality and personal preferences had a particularly direct influence on the nature of government and policy during these years. He was a monarch of commitment, vigour and vision. But whether the ends at which he aimed, and the methods he adopted to pursue them, were good or bad continues to divide historians just as it divided Charles's contemporaries.

Questions

1. What were Charles I's aims in government during the 1630s, and how successfully did he achieve them?
2. Why did Charles I's secular policies during the personal rule prove so controversial?

ANALYSIS (2): TO WHAT EXTENT, AND WHY, WERE THE REFORMS OF LAUD UNPOPULAR?

When Archbishop Abbot died in August 1633, Charles immediately appointed the Bishop of London, William Laud, to succeed him, despite James I's perceptive warning that Laud had 'a restless spirit' and could not 'see when matters are well'.[11] Together, Charles and the new Archbishop promoted a series of reforms within the Church which formed a coherent and integrated package. There was, as Peter Lake has written, 'a distinctive Laudian style' based upon 'a coherent view of true religion and ecclesiastical order'.[12] In order to understand reactions to these reforms, and the extent of their popularity, the salient features of this 'Laudian style' must first be briefly sketched.

The central element of Laud's reforms was a deep commitment to a ceremonial style of worship summed up by the phrase 'the beauty of holiness'. Laud was one of those 'ceremonialists' who had formed one strand within the Church ever since the Elizabethan Settlement. Like such earlier divines as Hooker, Whitgift and Lancelot Andrewes, he regarded the sacraments as the essence of worship, and believed passionately in the need for dignity and decency in church services. In most churches until the 1630s, the eucharist was celebrated around a plain 'communion table' set in the middle of the church. By contrast, Laud wanted the altar to stand at the east end of the chancel and to be railed in to prevent desecration. He also wanted church fabric, which had often been neglected, to be restored and beautified in order to provide a proper setting for worship.

Laud's commitment to the sacraments was based on an anti-Calvinist theology that saw God's grace as universally available, and stressed the free will of individuals to attain or forfeit salvation as a result of their own actions. He rejected the doctrine of predestination because it appeared to make 'the God of all mercies to be the most fierce and unreasonable tyrant in the world'.[13] These ideas were not particularly novel in themselves. What was new was the fact that Laud – with Charles I's strong support – tried to ensure that the entire nation conformed to his preferred style of worship and wished to suppress alternatives. He launched a concerted attack on the voluntary religious activities that the 'godly' of Elizabethan and Jacobean England had been allowed to pursue in addition to the official church services. In 1633 bishops were instructed to ensure that only ministers of parishes preached sermons, and that 'afternoon sermons be turned into catechising.'[14] That same year, Laud secured the suppression of the Feoffees for Impropriations, a group of clergy and laity who bought back tithes impropriated to laymen and used them to fund godly lecturers.

These reforms were accompanied by an aggressive assertion of the authority and status of the clergy. Laud believed that bishops and archbishops exercised their office by divine right, and that they formed a completely separate 'order' rather than just another 'degree' of the clergy.[15] At both national and local levels, clergy were appointed to secular offices on an unprecedented scale: in 1636, for example, Bishop Juxon of London became the first clerical Lord Treasurer since the fifteenth century. Such appointments, together with concerted efforts to regain former Church lands alienated since the Reformation, appeared to encroach on lay interests, as did the attempts to remove the private pews of local nobility or gentry from many parish churches. By the mid-1630s, moreover, the Laudians had acquired a virtual monopoly on senior Church offices: instead of the diversity of the broad Jacobean Church, one particular group now held sway, determined to assert that theirs was the only legitimate pattern of belief and worship.

Not surprisingly, these reforms proved intensely controversial. Many found 'the beauty of holiness', with its emphasis on ceremony and the sacraments, all too reminiscent of Catholicism. They were alarmed at hints that Laud did not regard the break with Rome as irrevocable, and that he positioned the Church of England closer to the Church of Rome than to what he called 'Calvin's new fangled device at Geneva'.[16] The fact that his reforms coincided with a remarkable resurgence of Catholicism at Court – evident in several high-level conversions and the welcoming of papal agents for the first time since Mary Tudor's reign – further reinforced the view summed up by the Earl of Bedford that Laud was 'the little thief put into the window of the church to unlock the door to popery'.[17] There was also widespread resentment of Laud's suppression of practices that the godly regarded as the essence of their religious life, such as extra sermons on Sunday afternoons. There is little doubt that by the later 1630s Laud's reforms were widely and deeply unpopular, and this hostility took both overt and covert forms.

First, a few people expressed their objections in print. The most famous of these were William Prynne, Henry Burton and John Bastwick, who published pamphlets denouncing Laud and the bishops for encouraging popish practices within the Church. All three were brought before Star Chamber in June 1637, where they were convicted of libel, fined £5,000 each, imprisoned for life and condemned to have their ears cropped. Similarly savage penalties were imposed on Alexander Leighton in 1630 (when Laud was already a powerful figure as Bishop of London) and John Lilburne in 1638. These exemplary punishments not only helped to blacken Star Chamber's reputation but prompted considerable public demonstrations of sympathy with the victims.

Although these few individuals were very much the exception, there is some evidence that their opinions were widely shared but that many people, understandably, chose not to speak out. Often the evidence is tucked away in private correspondence, or in diaries, such as that in which Robert Woodford, the steward of Northampton, bemoaned the 'vayne ceremonyes' implemented by the 'favourers and p[ro]moters of sup[er]stition and idolatry'.[18] Some godly people found solace and solidarity in secret gatherings, like the circle that met at Lord Brooke's home at Warwick Castle.[19] A number of ministers found ways of quietly evading the demands of the Laudian bishops.[20] Other people took more drastic action: during the 1630s as a whole as many as 15,000 emigrated to New England for primarily religious reasons.[21] In all these different responses, the sense of grievance was unmistakable and it alone can explain the extraordinary venom of the attacks on Laud and his allies when Parliament reassembled in 1640.

There may, however, be a danger of over-registering hostility to the Laudian reforms and underrating their popularity. A godly, Bible-centred, non-Laudian form of piety often appealed disproportionately to the literate, and thus to those most likely to produce some kind of written record, or to sit in Parliament. It is also probable that those who were fundamentally content with the direction of policy, or just apathetic, were least likely to leave any evidence of their opinions. Certainly there are signs that Laudianism won some support at the universities of Oxford and, to a lesser extent, Cambridge, and that it was often to the younger generation that it exercised a particular appeal.[22]

More widely, it has been suggested that Laudian reforms struck a chord among some ordinary folk for whom godly Calvinism had never offered a sympathetic religious experience. For those who found the Calvinist doctrine of predestination harsh, and the biblicism of the godly inaccessible, Laudianism presented a style of worship that appealed to the senses and a more optimistic account of the possibility of salvation through the sacraments. Churchwardens' accounts, although they only survive patchily, suggest that there may have been some moves towards the beautification of church fabric and a more ceremonial style of worship, and as many as three-quarters of England's 9,000 parishes may have had altar rails by 1639. It is possible that this does not only reflect acquiescence to the energetic visitations of Laudian bishops; there may have been a positive welcoming of the reforms, particularly among those who harboured a fondness for pre-Reformation Catholicism.[23] But because the people in question were overwhelmingly non-literate, it is virtually impossible for us to measure how extensive such feelings were. It is also worth remembering that many people were ignorant of the finer points of theological debate, and were willing to go along with whatever the prevailing powers demanded at the time. Once the Laudian regime collapsed, the majority of parish churches saw their altar rails destroyed (or at least stored away) by 1641.

In a sense the real problem, as with Charles's secular policies, was not that Laudian reforms were universally unpopular but that they divided opinion. Some people may have viewed them positively, but for many others they represented a narrowing of legitimate practice and an unwelcome drive for 'unity through uniformity'. Significant numbers of clergy and laity ceased to feel welcome within the Church, and the delicate equilibrium of the Jacobean and Elizabethan Churches was upset. Small wonder that by 1640 many people looked back affectionately to the Church 'of Elizabeth and James'.[24] For in place of the broad spectrum of religious belief that had existed prior to 1625, Laudian reforms had produced a harsh and bitter polarisation.

Questions

1. How far did Laud's reforms constitute a break from previous practice within the Church of England?
2. To what extent do you agree with John Morrill's verdict that 'by 1640, Laud was the most hated man in England'?

SOURCES

1. THE CAROLINE COURT

Source A: Design for a new palace at Whitehall, by Inigo Jones's pupil and collaborator John Webb, c. 1637–9. The upper elevation would have faced on to St James's park, the lower on to the River Thames (see opposite).

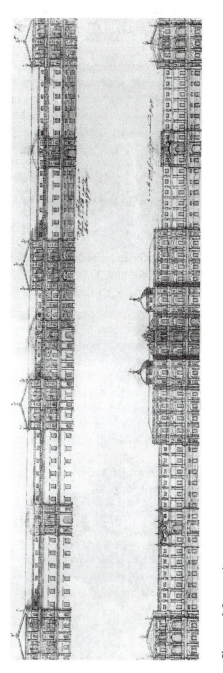

Chapter 6 Source A
By permission The Provost and Fellows of Worcester College, Oxford © Courtauld Institute of Art

Source B: Part of the text of William Davenant's *Salmacida Spolia*, a masque presented by the King and Queen's Majesties at Whitehall on 21 January 1640.

His Majesty out of his mercy and clemency . . . seeks by all means to reduce tempestuous and turbulent natures into a sweet calm of civil discord . . .

Chorus:
All that are harsh, all that are rude,
Are by your harmony subdu'd;
Yet so into obedience wrought,
As if not forc'd to it, but taught.

Source C: John Webb's design for the final scene of *Salmacida Spolia* (1640) (see opposite).

Source D: An extract from Charles I's proclamation of 28 July 1635 regulating touching for scrofula (the 'King's Evil').

Whereas heretofore the usual times of presenting such persons [i.e. those suffering from scrofula] to His Majestie for this purpose were Easter and Whitsontide . . . from henceforth the times shall be Easter and Michaelmas, as times more convenient, both for the temperature of the season, and in respect of any contagion which may happen in this neere accesse to His Majesties sacred person . . . And His Majestie doth further will . . . that all such . . . shall bring with them certificates under the hands of the parson, vicar or minister, and churchwardens . . . and under the hands and seales of one or more Justices of the Peace for . . . testifying . . . that they have not at any time before beene touched by the King, to the intent to be healed of that disease.

Source E: From the Venetian Ambassador's report to the Doge and Senate of Venice, 25 April 1625.

The King observes a rule of great decorum. The nobles do not enter his apartments in confusion as heretofore, but each rank has its appointed place and he has declared that he desires the rules and maxims of the late Queen Elizabeth . . . The King has also drawn up rules for himself, dividing the day from his very early rising, for prayers, exercises, audiences, business, eating and sleeping. It is said that he will set apart a day for public audience and he does not wish anyone to be introduced to him unless sent for.

Chapter 6 Source C
Devonshire Collection, Chatsworth. By permission of the Duke of Devonshire and the Chatsworth Settlement Trustees.
Photographic Survey, Courtauld Institute of Art.

Questions

*1. Read Source B.
   (i) Comment on its date. [2]
   (ii) Explain the significance of the phrase 'As if not forc'd to it,
        but taught'. [2]
2. What do Sources A, B and C tell us about Charles I's vision of
   monarchy? [6]
3. How would you imagine that Source D was received by the
   nation at large? [4]
4. How useful is Source E as a historical source? [3]
5. 'Conservative aims but a radical style'. Use these Sources and
   your wider knowledge to discuss this assessment of the
   Caroline Court. [8]

Worked answer

*1. *[These questions carry only a small number of marks, so answers
should be brief. It is important to focus precisely on the relevant date or
phrase and draw out its significance.]*

(i) It is very ironic that this masque, which emphasises the King's role in
imposing order upon chaos, was performed just as the personal rule was
collapsing. In June 1639, Charles I had led an unsuccessful campaign
against the Scots, and during the summer and autumn there had been
(for the first time) widespread refusal to pay Ship Money all over England.
Less than a month after *Salmacida Spolia* was performed, financial need
forced Charles to summon a new Parliament to meet on 13 April 1640.
That this masque was performed in such a context reveals something of
the unworldly atmosphere of the Caroline Court, and indicates how cut
off it had become from wider developments.

(ii) This phrase gives an indication of how Charles and his supporters saw
the reforms of the 1630s. They believed that the King's policies were
teaching his subjects new and better ways, and they saw the regime as
benignly didactic rather than coercive ('not forc'd to it'). Although this
optimistic view is echoed by some historians, notably Kevin Sharpe, it
would not have been shared by many of Charles's subjects, especially
those who suffered harsh penalties for their opposition to official policies.

SOURCES

2. WILLIAM LAUD AND THE CHURCH

Source F: From an open letter from Laud to Charles I, which formed the preface to William Laud, *A Relation of the Conference between William Laud . . . and Mr Fisher the Jesuit* (1639).

No one thing hath made conscientious men more wavering in their own minds . . . than the want of uniform and decent order in too many churches of the kingdom . . . These thoughts are they, and no other, which have made me labour so much as I have done for decency and an orderly settlement of the external worship of God in the Church . . . Ceremonies are the hedge that fences the substance of religion from all the indignities which profaneness and sacrilege too commonly put upon it.

Source G: From William Laud, *A Relation of the Conference between William Laud . . . and Mr Fisher the Jesuit* (1639).

The Protestants did not get that name by protesting against the Church of Rome, but by protesting . . . against her errors and superstitions. Do you but remove them from the Church of Rome, and our Protestation is ended, and the separation too.

Source H: Part of Laud's speech at the second trial of William Prynne, June 1637.

[The altar is] the greatest place of God's residence upon earth . . . I say the greatest, yea, greater than the pulpit; for there 'tis *hoc est corpus meum*, 'this is my body': but in the pulpit 'tis at most but *hoc est verbum meum*, 'this is my word'. And a greater reverence, no doubt, is due to the body than to the word of our Lord.

Source I: From the Impeachment Articles against Laud, presented to the House of Commons on 26 February 1641.

VII. That he [Laud] hath traitorously endeavoured to alter and subvert God's true religion by law established in this realm; and instead thereof, to set up popish superstition and idolatry; . . . He hath urged and enjoined divers popish and superstitious ceremonies, without any warrant of law; and hath cruelly persecuted those who have opposed the same, by corporal punishment and imprisonment . . .

X. He hath traitorously and wickedly endeavoured to reconcile the Church of England with the Church of Rome.

Source J: From *The Letany of John Bastwick* (1637).

Now I beseech you look upon the pride and ingratitude of [the bishops] . . . How magnificent and glorious will [Laud] be . . . when he goeth in state and in great power to Cambridge and Oxford in his metropolitical rogation and perambulation, and with a rod in his hand . . . to whip those naughty scholars, that will not learn their lessons of conformity . . . nor will not cringe to the altar, nor turn their faces to the East, nor worship the communion table . . . For the Church is now as full of ceremonies, as a dog is full of fleas.

Questions

1. (i) Read Source H. Explain the significance of the phrases 'this is my body', and 'the body . . . of our Lord'. [2]
   (ii) Read Source J. Explain the term 'metropolitical rogation and perambulation'. [2]
2. How convincing do you find Source F as a justification for Laud's policies? [3]
3. How far do Sources I and J present similar or different charges against Laud? [4]
*4. To what extent do Sources F, G and H provide evidence to support the charges in Sources I and J? [7]
5. 'A sincere but much misunderstood man'. Is this a fair assessment of Laud? Refer to these Sources and your wider knowledge in your answer. [7]

Worked answer

*4. *[An effective way to approach this question is to compare the attitudes evident in Laud's own writings with those attributed to him by his critics, and assess how far these are similar or different.]*

Three accusations are expressed particularly strongly in one or both of Sources I and J. First, Source I denounces Laud for promoting 'divers popish and superstitious ceremonies', while Source J laments that the Church is 'full of ceremonies'. There is much evidence to support this: in Source F, Laud describes ceremonies as a vital fence for the 'substance of religion' and in Source H he identifies the sacrament of the eucharist as the most sacred part of the service. The crucial issue here is not whether Laud promoted ceremonies as such, but whether that was a good thing or not. For Laud, ceremonies were vital to ensure a 'uniform and decent order' in worship (Source F), whereas to his opponents they were 'popish' (Source I). Indeed, given that what he called 'decency'

(Source F) was essentially the same as what they called 'idolatry' (Source I), an unbridgeable gulf opened up between them.

Second, Laud is accused of seeking to 'reconcile the Church of England with the Church of Rome' (Source I). Source G certainly indicates that he did not regard the break from Rome as irrevocable, and the logic of his argument is that if Rome were cleansed of 'errors and superstitions' then a reunion was possible. Source H does not necessarily prove that Laud accepted the Catholic doctrine of transubstantiation, whereby during the mass the bread and wine were believed physically to become the body and blood of Christ. But his words ('this is my body', 'the body . . . of our Lord') do not rule out such a belief, and they play down the view – widely held among English Protestants in this period – that the eucharist was a commemoration of the Last Supper. To many, Source H would have seemed dangerously 'popish'.

Third, there is the more general charge that Laud had aggrandised himself and the bishops. This point is less obviously apparent in the first three Sources. However, some contemporaries would have seen the major role that Laud took in Star Chamber (Source H) as evidence of the arrogance and excessive prominence within royal counsels so vehemently denounced in Source J.

7

IRELAND UNDER SIR THOMAS WENTWORTH, EARL OF STRAFFORD

BACKGROUND NARRATIVE

At the age of thirty-nine, Sir Thomas Wentworth was appointed Lord Deputy of Ireland on 12 January 1632. This promotion followed a period of three years as President of the Council of the North, an office from which he compelled respect for the authority of the Crown by imprisoning recalcitrant gentry such as Henry Bellasys and Sir David Foulis. Yet this picture of Wentworth as a loyal servant of the Crown apparently contrasts with his actions in the 1620s, not least his refusal in 1627 to pay the Forced Loan (for which he was imprisoned) and his insistence in the Parliament of 1628 that 'unless we [i.e. members of the political nation] be secured in our liberties, we cannot give'.[1] Some historians have therefore argued that by becoming an agent of the Crown Wentworth was guilty of gross apostasy. However, this Whig interpretation has been criticised by those who see England's political order in the early seventeenth century as an organically united commonwealth – in other words, they argue that 'sides' did not exist – and by research which suggests that Wentworth did not fundamentally change his principles in 1629.

Wentworth arrived in Dublin on 23 July 1633 determined upon firm government from the centre intended to break through self-interested obstructionism, a policy that he and Laud referred to in their letters as 'Thorough'. The new Lord Deputy employed a number of devices in order to achieve this end, especially the prerogative machinery of government such as the Commission for Defective Titles, High Commission and Castle Chamber (the Irish equivalent to the English Star Chamber). Success was also facilitated by exploitation of existing rivalries between the three main elements in Ireland: the Gaelic Irish, Old English and New English. The first two, although both Catholic, were antagonistic towards each other because the Old English, since the time of the Conquest, had usurped much of the territory of the indigenous Gaelic population. Recent colonisation had been undertaken by the so-called New English, Protestant English and Scots who had been granted land in Ireland. The New English, recognising that they could only succeed by displacing the Old English, therefore denigrated the latter as being in league with the Pope and as gun-runners to the Gaelic Irish. This in turn prompted the Old English to seek statutory recognition of their property titles, formally articulated in the Graces in 1628, though never fully granted.

In 1639 Wentworth was recalled from Ireland in order to shore up the tottering personal rule of Charles I. Newly elevated to the earldom of Strafford and lord lieutenancy of Ireland (January 1640), and emboldened by the success of the first session of the Irish Parliament, March–June 1640, Strafford now advised the King to call a Parliament in England. When this so-called Short Parliament failed to provide supply for the anticipated Second Bishops' War, Strafford nevertheless urged an immediate invasion of Scotland and argued that funds should be collected by force. The Second Bishops' War proved disastrous, royal forces suffering defeat at the Battle of Newburn on 28 August 1640 – the first time the Scots had enjoyed victory over the English since Bannockburn in 1314. Effectively bankrupt, Charles was therefore obliged to call in November 1640 the Long Parliament. From this platform, with support from Irish and Scottish elements, MPs proceeded to attack the Lord Lieutenant, accusing him of 'a great and dangerous treason'.[2] However, partly because of the effectiveness of his own defence and partly because of unease at Pym's methods, the attempt to impeach Strafford ran into difficulty. Thus, the leaders of the opposition element in the Commons resorted to the use of attainder, a legislative procedure which simply enacted that Strafford's actions were treasonable. Ultimately the King was obliged to give his assent to the Attainder Bill on 10 May 1641. Strafford was executed two days later.

ANALYSIS: BY WHAT METHODS, AND WITH WHAT DEGREE OF SUCCESS, DID SIR THOMAS WENTWORTH GOVERN IRELAND?

A flurry of biographies in the 1930s established what for a long time remained as the orthodox view of Sir Thomas Wentworth's government as Lord Deputy of Ireland.[3] These authors presented Wentworth as being 'efficient and incorruptible and . . . determined to maintain the highest possible ideal of government'.[4] For instance, to C. V. Wedgwood here was a 'simple and generous man . . . fearless in the pursuit of what he believed to be right'.[5] From this perspective Wentworth's ultimate failure and destruction are thus explicable in part because of the cunning and determination of his adversaries and in part because the very virtues which became him as a man also weakened him as a politician. However, this view of Wentworth was altered by the research undertaken by H. Kearney and J. P. Cooper in the 1950s. These historians demonstrated that Wentworth, far from being the selfless servant of the Crown, accepted the deputyship at least partly for reasons of profit: enjoying an annual income of £13,000, he was certainly one of the richest men in Britain. Kearney argues that the instruments of 'Thorough' were not of Wentworth's making – rather, that he merely 'carried on in the way that his predecessors, Chichester, Grandison and Falkland had done, creating nothing but destroying nothing'. He concludes that 'the seeds of eventual disaster lay within Wentworth's financial achievements' and that his religious policy was 'completely misconceived' and 'destined to arouse grave discontent'.[6] This interpretation was taken further by T. Ranger, his findings forcing him to the conclusion that Wentworth was 'above all, a man who brought disaster'.[7] There has been no serious recent attempt either to elaborate or to revise this picture of Charles I's minister, persuading J. F. Merritt to castigate 'English historians [for failing] to make systematic use of the sprawling [Wentworth] correspondence from the 1630s'.[8]

All historians agree that Lord Deputy Wentworth had at least two main aims, namely to ensure that the Irish administration became financially independent of England and that the fortunes of the Protestant Church in Ireland were not only revived, but refashioned along the same lines as those delineated by Laud for the English Church.

In desperate need of supply, Wentworth called a Parliament in 1634. He prepared carefully, recommending particular candidates and, in the case of Dublin, forcibly preventing the town council from electing candidates of whom he did not approve. By such means he created a Deputy's party which he employed as a device to hold the balance between the two main groups, the Catholic Old English and the Protestant New English. 'The truth is', wrote Wentworth to Secretary Coke in January 1633, 'we must there [i.e. in the forthcoming Parliament] bow and govern the native by the planter and the planter by the native.'[9] Circumstance aided Wentworth in this policy of divide and rule because, as Kearney has observed, 'neither Old English nor New English dared give the impression of hostility for fear the Deputy would throw his weight upon the opposite side'.[10] Thus, by voting for the six subsidies demanded by Wentworth (a total of £120,000), the Old English MPs believed that they could avoid any renewed levy of recusancy fines and henceforth realistically expect statutory confirmation of the Graces.[11] However, having obtained the subsidies, the Lord Deputy then failed to grant fully the Graces, 'refusing [the Old English] their two darling Articles' (the two Graces which affected land tenure).[12] Subsequently, by leaning upon the support of the New English, Wentworth was able to ride out the 'peevishness' of the 'Popish Party [i.e. the Old English]'.[13]

Yet parliamentary supply could never be anything other than a short-term palliative. Nor could the levy of fines provide any long-term financial security, even when they amounted to the huge sum of £70,000 which the Corporation of London was obliged to pay after it was found guilty of a breach in its contract relating to a grant of land in Londonderry. Thus, Wentworth set about increasing revenues from Crown lands. He employed three methods in particular towards achieving this end. First, he initiated the plantation of new areas. Second, he sought to raise rents upon the discovery of Crown titles. Finally, the Lord Deputy desired the Crown fully to exploit its fiscal feudal devices, an ambition which he significantly implemented by vigorously applying prerogative machinery of state, especially the Court of Wards and, from 1634, the Commission for Defective Titles, established 'for converting all doubtful and confused claims to land into tenures from the Crown so that the royal revenues would be increased at the expense of the landowners in Ireland'.[14] Wentworth had no hesitation in launching punitive proceedings against an individual who had been making a profit out of the existing confusion of tenures. On this charge Lord Balfour, a leading Protestant, was fined £200 and Vice-Treasurer Mountnorris (see below) was compelled to return an estate he had acquired by dubious means. Though a landowner whose title was confirmed by the Commission would henceforth be safe from future legal claims against his tenure, he remained liable to duties levied by the Crown, not least those which fell under the auspices of the Court of Wards.[15] Between 1630 and 1640 the Court of Wards brought in a total income of £69,370.[16]

The most dramatic example of the implementation of these devices comes from the summer of 1635 when Wentworth decided to 'plant'

Connacht, the province on the west of Ireland composed of the counties of Leitrim, Sligo, Mayo, Roscommon and Galway. At the head of the Commission for Defective Titles, Wentworth, in the words of Christopher Wandesford, a close friend of the Lord Deputy, intended 'the King's title [to be] found to a principal part of the county of Connaught'.[17] Thereafter, land which was successfully claimed by the Crown was to be granted to settlers who would 'industriously attend their own undertakings' and 'breed civility'.[18] This policy enjoyed immediate success in the counties of Sligo, Mayo and Roscommon, a consequence of the careful selection of jurors empanelled to consider the titles to land combined with a general recognition by the existing tenants that a failure to resist meant that it was more likely that land would be regranted to present incumbents – albeit on a rather more expensive form of tenure – rather than expropriated and granted to planters. However, Wentworth encountered substantial resistance in his attempt to plant Galway, a county in which the dominant landowner was Richard de Burgh, Earl of Clanricarde, a significant force among the Old English. The Galway jury contained no fewer than ten of Clanricarde's relatives and thus 'most obstinately and perversely refused to find for his Majesty'.[19] Wentworth, increasingly under attack from Clanricarde's allies at Court in England, now showed his true mettle. He fined the sheriff who had empanelled the jury and although he later died in prison, nevertheless collected the fine; he also summoned the jurors before the Castle Chamber, imprisoned and fined them for giving a wrong verdict and, finally, moved a garrison into Galway.

Above all, in order to enhance the finances of the Crown, Wentworth was determined to ensure that the regime benefited fully from the growth in trade, a consequence of the termination of the wars against France and Spain. Thus, he better organised the naval guard for the Irish coasts and in so doing substantially reduced the incidence of piracy, especially after having smoked out a significant nest of sea robbers from their base in the Isle of Man. The Lord Deputy also greatly modified the process relating to the export of wool, enforcing a revised licensing system combined with a more efficient management of the ports which together significantly reduced the opportunities for corruption. Finally, he devised a new Book of Rates in 1632 and proceeded successfully to alter the terms and conditions relating to the collection of customs and, in so doing, significantly enhanced the income derived from this source. Indeed, during the period 1636–1637 the profits from the customs farm – administration of the customs had been leased ('farmed') to merchant contractors – were almost equal to the total yield for 1632–1633.

Meanwhile, Wentworth set about implementing his religious programme. Central to this was his belief that the interests of the Protestant

Church in Ireland were best served by avoiding attacks upon the Catholics (in case this prompted rebellion) until the Protestant Church had been strengthened. 'To attempt [the conversion of Ireland]', wrote Wentworth to Laud, 'before the decays of the material churches be repaired, and able clergy be provided, that so there might be both wherewith to receive, instruct and keep the people, were as a man going to warfare without ammunition or arms.'[20] In his quest to further the interests of the Protestant Church the Lord Deputy therefore set about restoring tithes and Church lands which had been usurped by laymen. He also sought to bring its articles of religion, canons and liturgical practices much more closely into line with English practice as fashioned by Archbishop Laud.

This was effected by a variety of methods. First, he set about altering the personnel of the Church. The Archbishop of Armagh, James Ussher, found himself sidelined because he had demonstrated sympathy with that element antagonistic to the anti-Calvinists. Meanwhile, Wentworth secured the appointment of John Bramhall and Henry Leslie as bishops of Derry and Down, respectively, men whom he could rely upon to do his bidding. He also moved against those bishops who were dependent upon great landowners so that by 1640 the episcopate of the Church of Ireland had very significantly changed its character. Then, on the basis that it had become a centre for Puritan teaching, Robert Ussher was replaced as Provost of Trinity College, Dublin by William Chappell, a nominee of Wentworth. Second, just as he had done in order to enhance the finances of the Crown, the Lord Deputy used coercion and intimidation in his quest to implement his religious programme. For instance, when Convocation (an assembly of clergy that met at the same time as Parliament) baulked at the demand that it impose the Thirty-Nine Articles and Canons of the English Church upon the Irish Church, the Lord Deputy won the day by letting it be known that 'I hold it not fit nor will suffer that the Articles of the Church of England be disputed'. Ominously, he also sought information about 'how each man gives his vote'.[21] Nor did Wentworth hesitate in employing the prerogative courts in the interests of the Irish Church. Thus, in his quest to force the Earl of Cork to disgorge impropriated properties, the Earl was summoned before the Court of Castle Chamber. A compromise agreement was finally reached in April 1636 whereby Cork paid a fine of £15,000. The Lord Deputy also reinstituted the Court of High Commission. Composed of a group of bishops with powers either to fine or imprison, this court sat frequently over the course of the next five years. In 1635 it deprived five ministers in the diocese of Down and County for refusing to subscribe to the Canons.

In the short term, in financial and religious respects, Wentworth's achievement was spectacular. Indeed, his handling of the Irish economy appears to have been extraordinarily successful. Having inherited a debt of £76,000 and a gap between ordinary revenue and ordinary expenditure which amounted to £20,000, within five years revenues were in excess of expenditure and the debt had been paid off. By the end of the 1630s revenues had been doubled to about £80,000 a year. For the first time since the later Middle Ages, the Irish Exchequer did not need to seek contributions from either the English government or from Irish Parliaments. Moreover, by the end of the 1630s Wentworth had facilitated the return of significant amounts of land to the Church and, as observed by Kearney, created conditions in which 'the Laudian movement [in Ireland] came nearer to apparent success than it did in either England or Scotland'.[22] Where Wentworth had thus far failed, most notably in his avowed intention to populate Galway 'thoroughly with English and Protestants', it seemed that there was time yet in which to find able and industrious colonists willing to come to Ireland from England.[23]

Yet this achievement had been purchased at enormous political cost. Powerful individuals, Old English and New English, had been disaffected not only by Wentworth's general policies but by heavy-handed, ill-considered actions. For instance, Clanricarde had to suffer an attack upon his title to his estates and weather a number of personal affronts such as the Lord Deputy casting 'himself in his riding boots upon [Clanricarde's] very rich beds'.[24] Similarly, Cork was outraged by Wentworth's insensitive insistence that he remove from its prominent position in St Patrick's Cathedral the expensive Cork family tomb. Lord Mountnorris, Vice-Treasurer and leading customs farmer who was undoubtedly mulcting the regime for his own ends – he had received about £20,000 from the customs farm in 1635 – was another of the New English whom Wentworth determined to proceed against. Yet it was on very doubtful grounds that the Lord Deputy court-martialled Mountnorris and had him condemned to death, though the sentence was never carried out. In these ways Wentworth made some very dangerous enemies, not least because they had allies at the English Court who mobilised opinion against him to such an extent that in 1636 he was obliged to return to England to defend his interests.

All elements, Old English, New English and Gaelic Irish – and indeed Scots resident in Ireland who, caught up in the Anglo-Scottish crisis of the late 1630s, found themselves proceeded against – were provided with a common reason to detest Wentworth, not least because each was threatened by large-scale changes in the ownership of land. Perhaps yet more damaging to the prospect of future stable government in Ireland, however, was the fact that the natural allies of the administration, the New English, had in general been utterly alienated, partly by Wentworth's land and customs farming policies but also because Catholics were appeased whilst Protestants were proceeded against.

Blinded by overconfidence, Wentworth could not see that many in Ireland were thus 'sheathing in flattering looks the deadly knife'.[25] Recalled to England in April 1640 in order to shore up the personal rule, Wentworth henceforth had to face simultaneous attacks upon his authority from, on the one hand, the unnatural, but predictable, alliance that now formed among the three main elements in Irish society – the New English, the Old English and the Gaelic Irish – and, on the other hand, the anti-Wentworth faction at Court. It proved an insuperable combination. He was therefore impeached and, after skilfully defending himself at his trial, subsequently attainted. He was executed on 12 May 1641.

Questions

1. 'Against all the odds he achieved extraordinary success.' How far do you agree with this assessment of Strafford in the 1630s?
2. What were the problems involved in governing Ireland in the 1630s and how effectively were they overcome by Strafford?

SOURCES

1. STRAFFORD'S GOVERNMENT

Source A: From a speech by Strafford to the Council of the North, 30 December 1628.

Subjects ought, with solicitous eyes of jealousy, to watch over the Prerogatives of a Crown. The authority of a King is the keystone which closeth up the arch of order and government, which contains each part in due relation to the whole, and which once shaken, infirmed, all the frame falls together into a confused heap of foundation and battlement . . . I do here offer myself [as] an instrument for good in every man's hand.

Source B: Strafford to one of his agents at the English Court, 1635.

I do not serve the King out of the ordinary ends that the servants of great princes attend with them; great wealth I covet not; greater powers than are already entrusted to me by my master I do not desire. I wish much rather abilities to discharge those I have, as becomes me, than any of those I have not. Again I serve not for reward, having received much more than I shall ever be able to deserve.

Source C: Strafford's advice to Charles, 5 May 1640.

Go on with a vigorous war, as you first designed, loosed and absolved from all rules of government, being reduced to extreme necessity, everything is to be done that power might admit, and that you are to do. They [i.e. the Short Parliament] refusing, you are acquitted towards God and man, you have an army in Ireland you may employ here to reduce this kingdom.

Source D: The third Article of Strafford's impeachment, 1641.

That the said Earl being Lord Deputy of that Realm [i.e. Ireland] sought to bring His Majesty's liege subjects of that kingdom into dislike of His Majesty's government, and intending the subversion of the Fundamental Laws and government of that Realm, and the destruction of His Majesty's liege – people there did ... declare and publish that Ireland was a conquered nation and that the King might do with [the Irish] what he pleased.

Questions

1. Read Sources C and D. Comment upon the phrases 'this kingdom' and 'conquered nation'. [4]
2. How useful do you consider Source A for a historian researching the political outlook of Wentworth? [4]
*3. Read Source B. With reference to the content of this Source and your own knowledge, how reliable do you consider this letter for a historian researching the motives of Strafford? [5]
4. How far do Sources C and D indicate that Strafford as Lord Deputy of Ireland was simply attempting to implement his philosophy of government as outlined in Source A? [5]
5. To what extent do these Sources and your own knowledge suggest that, as Lord Deputy in Ireland, Strafford was 'an instrument for good' (Source A)? [7]

Worked answer

*3. *[It is important to balance references to the content of the Source with knowledge obtained from wider reading.]*

Strafford's assertion that he did 'not desire' 'great wealth' or 'greater powers' – the 'ordinary ends' aimed at by 'servants of great princes' – is so self-deprecating that it arouses deep suspicion as to his real purpose in writing this letter. Indeed, he even questions whether his abilities are sufficient to handle the responsibilities of his position. Thus, it seems probable that this letter was intended in particular to appease his critics at Court and, as such, it is only really reliable as an example of the statecraft of Strafford. In fact, not only did Strafford become one of the richest men in Britain during the 1630s but the pattern of his career suggests that he enjoyed the prestige of high office and did indeed seek 'greater powers'. Certainly, his quest for an earldom was a particular ambition for much of the 1630s.

SOURCES

2. THE TRIAL OF STRAFFORD, 1641

Source E: Strafford's last speech in his defence, 13 April 1641.

It is now full two hundred and forty years since any man was touched for this alleged crime to this height before myself. Let us not awaken those sleeping lions to our destruction by taking up a few musty records that have lain by the walls for so many ages, forgotten or neglected. My Lords, what is my present misfortune may be forever yours! It is not the smallest part of my grief that not the crime of treason, but my other sins, which are exceeding many, have brought me to this bar; and, except your Lordships' wisdom provide against it, the shedding of my blood may make way for the tracing of yours. You, your estates, your posterity, lie at stake.

Source F: From a speech of John Pym on 13 April 1641, responding to Strafford.

Nothing can be more equal than that he [i.e. Strafford] should perish by the justice of the law which he would have subverted; neither will this be a new way of blood. There are marks enough to trace this law [i.e. attainder] to the very original of this kingdom; and if it hath not been put into execution, as he alleged, this 240 years, it was not for want of law, but all that time hath not bred a man bold enough to commit such crimes as these, which is a circumstance much aggravating his offence, and making him no less liable to punishment, because he is the only man that, in so long a time, had ventured upon such a treason as this.

Source G: From Clarendon's *History*. (Edward Hyde, Earl of Clarendon commenced his *History* in 1646. He was present in London until 1642, by which time he had become a constitutional royalist.)

Multitudes of people came down to Westminster and crowded about the House of Peers, exclaiming with great outcries, that 'they would have justice'; and publicly reading the names of those who had dissented from that bill in the House of Commons as enemies to their country; and as any Lord passed by, called, Justice, Justice with great rudeness and insolence pressing upon and thrusting those Lords whom they suspected not to favour that bill . . . This unheard of act of insolence and sedition continued so many days, till many Lords grew really so apprehensive of having their brains beaten out that they absented themselves from the House and others . . . changed their minds. And so in an afternoon, when of the fourscore who had been present at the trial there were only six and forty Lords in the House, the good people still crying at the doors for Justice, they put the bill to the question, and, eleven Lords only dissenting, it passed that House and was ready for the King's assent.

Questions

1. Read Source F. Comment upon 'this law [i.e. attainder]'. [2]
2. Read Sources E and F. How convincing is Pym's attempt to refute the argument put forward by Strafford? [6]
3. Read Source E. With reference to tone and language, how effective do you consider this part of Strafford's speech? [6]
4. Read Sources E and G. In what ways does Source G support the predictions offered by Strafford? [4]
*5. How useful is Source G for the historian researching into the motivation of those peers who voted for the attainder of Strafford? [6]

Worked answer

*5. *[It is important to recognise ways in which the Source is useful and ways in which it is misleading. Cross-reference with other Sources where this is possible.]*

On the one hand, this is of use to a historian in a number of ways. First, Clarendon offers precise statistical information. He informs us that there were 'six and forty Lords in the House', of whom 'eleven' refrained from giving their assent to the Bill of Attainder. Second, Clarendon reports that those who 'absented themselves' or 'changed their minds' did so because they were fearful of 'having their brains beaten out', an observation which suggests that the arguments like those related in Sources E and F ultimately counted for little. Indeed, it is useful to learn that members of the non-political nation could affect political events in such a dramatic way and that they appear to have been informed and inspired by 'reading the names of those who had dissented from that bill in the House of Commons', the so-called Straffordians. It also seems to be the case that Clarendon witnessed these events first hand, reporting the mantra of the mob, 'Justice, Justice'.

On the other hand, Clarendon is clearly guilty of hyperbole. The 'people' are alleged to have behaved with 'great rudeness', 'insolence' (employed twice) and 'sedition', 'pressing upon' and 'thrusting' the Lords they thought were sympathetic to Strafford. It follows, therefore, that Clarendon, as a supporter of impeachment but not attainder of Strafford, could be exaggerating the role of the mob in order to provide a justification for the Lords' resort to such drastic action. Finally, this account would also have been more useful to the historian if Clarendon had given some numerical estimate of what, in his eyes, were 'great multitudes' and offered some detail as to what sort of 'people' composed the mob.

8

THE COMING OF
CIVIL WAR

BACKGROUND NARRATIVE

Historians have been unable to agree upon the origins of the English
Civil War, not least because of the peculiarly chaotic nature of the
five-year period immediately preceding the outbreak of hostilities in
England in 1642.

Even as England continued to bask in what one contemporary
described as 'the most serene, quiet and halcyon days that could
possibly be imagined', royal authority in Scotland was experiencing
serious assault.[1] Indeed, Charles I's determined attempt to impose a
new Prayer Book upon his northern subjects in 1637, having initially
met with resistance, ultimately induced outright rebellion when in
November 1638 the Glasgow Assembly abolished bishops in Scotland.
In 1639, and again in 1640, the King therefore mobilised resources to
fight the Scots only to find his efforts fatally weakened by leading
members of the English political nation whose sympathies for the
Scots were greater than their support for Charles. Unsurprisingly,
therefore, especially since the Short Parliament of April–May 1640
had been dissolved without offering any supply, the royal army
was routed at the Battle of Newburn on 28 August. Having lost the
Bishops' Wars and henceforth obliged to host an army of occupation,
Charles called what has become known as the Long Parliament in
November 1640.

There occurred over the course of the next eighteen months a polarisation of allegiances among MPs in the Long Parliament so that the King was eventually provided with a party. This process took place for a number of reasons, including: growing resentment among some MPs over Scottish interference in English affairs; deepening religious differences; and, above all, from October 1641, acrimonious debate over how to deal with the rebellion in Ireland. The rising of the Catholic Irish posed with acute urgency the question of the King's military authority and in so doing precipitated the armed confrontation of King and Parliament.

ANALYSIS (1): WAS THE OUTBREAK OF THE ENGLISH CIVIL WAR A CONSEQUENCE OF A CRISIS OF MULTIPLE KINGDOMS, 1637–1642?

Noting the problems encountered by composite monarchies like those of Spain and the Holy Roman Empire, Conrad Russell has developed a thesis that the English Civil War was the culmination of a crisis of multiple kingship, of the constant 'billiard-ball effect of each of the kingdoms on the affairs of the others'.[2] In other words, England's collapse was a result of the ways in which events in Scotland and Ireland impinged upon Charles I's largest, and apparently most stable, kingdom. Thus, the main ingredients for civil war – namely, a critical assault upon the majesty of monarchy, the formation of distinct political factions or sides, the failure of those factions to negotiate away their differences and the appearance on the political stage of an ideological issue sufficient to drive members of those factions to take up arms – were in effect injected into the English political system as a consequence of the multiple kingdom crisis ignited by the Scottish Prayer Book Rebellion of 1637. Russell acknowledges that there was combustible material in England but he argues that it was not of the sort that would combust spontaneously. A match had to be offered.

What follows is an attempt to outline Russell's position, though it should be borne in mind that his 'multiple kingdom' explanation for the outbreak of the English Civil War has been by no means universally accepted. For example, Ann Hughes has criticised Russell for giving 'the Scots more credit for initiating developments than does David Stevenson, the specialist historian of Scotland'.[3] John Morrill has also noticed that 'at times Russell seems to let the Scottish tail wag the English dog'. More particularly, Morrill has argued that Russell 'understates the explosive power of English puritanism to generate a national movement ready to fight the king, and, in direct response to puritan militancy, a national movement ready to join a discredited king'.[4]

According to Russell, the outbreak of civil war in England was facilitated by 'the problem of diminished majesty', or, as Lord Brooke put it, 'the courage almost to despite [i.e. criticise] to his [i.e. the King's] face'.[5] This development was encouraged by the existence of substantial dissident elements within England and the planted (i.e. Protestant) population in Ireland whose natural sympathies lay with the Scots. The harder that the King pressed against the Scots the more the dissident elements made common cause. Indeed, even before the Scottish riots of July 1637 Eleazar Borthwick, the London agent of the Scottish opposition group, had carried to Scotland messages of support and encouragement from English groups. Consequently, a probable reason for the King's decision not to call a Parliament in 1639 – the first occasion that a monarch of England had not called a Parliament during a time of war since 1323 – was because of a fear that Covenanter propaganda circulating in England had whipped up a dangerous quantity of support for the Scottish rebels. 'You will not believe how heartily your cause is wished to succeed [here in England] amongst the nobility, gentry and commonality,' wrote Sir John Clotworthy to a Scottish contact in 1638. He went on to remark that there were some forty or fifty 'leading persons' among the English political nation who were considering finding 'an America in Scotland'.[6] Equally, the Short Parliament of April–May 1640 was dissolved peremptorily and without providing supply for the Second Bishops' War largely because Charles feared that the Commons were preparing a declaration of sympathy with the Scots.

Simultaneously, the presence of Scots in Ulster was seriously destabilising Strafford's regime in Ireland. Professing support for their Covenanting brethren, the Ulster Scots proceeded to arm themselves and some set sail for Scotland. This attitude persuaded Strafford to post additional troops in Ulster and enforce the Black Oath, according to which Scots in Ireland were to abjure the Covenant. However, the main effect of this was further to encourage flight to Scotland. Henceforth, not only was the Covenanters' regime in Scotland made yet more resilient but the economy of Ulster was seriously destabilised because the 'great numbers' leaving for Scotland took with them 'their horses, cows, sheep and what else they have, and leave their corn standing in the ground'.[7]

Charles, by attempting to mobilise the resources of Ireland and England in order to put down the rebellion in his northern kingdom, ensured that the crisis took on a truly British dimension. Indeed, the immediate effect of a royal scheme of 1639 which encouraged the invasion of Scotland by a force raised and led by the Catholic Earl of Antrim, head of that clan who were Macdonnells in Ireland and Macdonalds in Scotland, ancient rivals of clan Campbell, was to push the Earl of Argyll, the Protestant head of clan Campbell, into the arms of the Covenanters. Similarly, Strafford's plan to quell the Covenanters by raising an Irish, largely Catholic, army of 8,000 men and 1,000 horse over the winter of 1639–1640 had enormous political consequences in that it deepened the existing Scottish interest in securing Protestant ascendancy in Ireland and frightened many popish-fearing Englishmen into supporting the Scots. In England, the King's decision to mobilise armies in the First and Second Bishops' Wars forced men to consider their position, encouraged the growing polarisation of English opinion between pro- and anti-Scots sentiments and generally galvanised the recalcitrants across England. 'The people in England in general abhorred [the Bishops' Wars] as a design to enslave both nations,' observed one commentator, who went on to conclude that the English 'loved the Scots as brothers prosecuted by that same wicked power'.[8]

Thus, the nature of events from 1637 encouraged the dissident groups in the three kingdoms into undertaking positive and sustained collusion, a development which is particularly discernible along the Anglo-Scottish axis. For instance, when Lords Saye and Brooke refused to take an oath of allegiance to Charles in May 1639 they were probably steeled to do so because of links forged with the Covenanters. Ultimately, the English opponents of Charles appreciated that if the Scots invaded England, established themselves as an occupying force and thereafter demanded financial reparation, then Charles would be compelled to call an English Parliament from which they could seek to redress the accumulated grievances of the personal rule. Therefore, the English dissidents probably colluded with the Scots to the extent that the rebels were encouraged to invade in August 1640. Indeed, recent research by Peter Donald has led him to conclude that in 1640 a substantial element of the English political nation was fully prepared 'to show solidarity with the Covenanters in their invasion, even to the point of taking arms against the King if necessary. There was, as it were, an "army plot" devised against Charles I which predated by several months the scheme in which he was involved against the Long Parliament.'[9] As the Scots crossed the border the leading English dissidents presented Charles with the Petition of Twelve Peers, requesting, among other things, that he 'summon a Parliament within some short and convenient time'.[10] Meanwhile, from the Scots' point of view, it was in their interests that Charles fulfil this demand because any terms of settlement they agreed with the King were likely to be short-lived unless guaranteed by an English Parliament. Indeed, the Scots were probably correct to fear that Charles, by making concessions to his English opponents, could yet wage a Third Bishops' War.

Collusion became open collaboration after the meeting of the Long Parliament in November 1640. John Clotworthy, a leading member of the anti-Strafford faction, became the principal intermediary between the English, Scottish and Irish malcontents. Having attempted a British response to the Scottish crisis, Strafford was thus brought to trial in England at the suit of all three kingdoms. An Irish Remonstrance presented to the Long Parliament provided sufficient political ammunition to initiate impeachment proceedings, though the eventual resort to the use of attainder induced a dangerously destabilising polarisation of opinion. Lord Digby's lament that they were 'committing murder with the sword of justice' was met with Essex's dour insistence that 'stone dead hath no fellow'.[11] Meanwhile, having abolished episcopacy in Scotland, the Covenanters successfully pressed – though only in the first instance – the root-and-branch petition in London.

Collaboration between opponents of Charles was made yet more effective by their direct copying of each other's successful procedures. Thus, the Scottish National Covenant of February 1638 was an important influence upon the English Protestation of May 1641. Similarly, the Long Parliament's quest to obtain a Triennial Act followed almost twelve months after the Scots had already done the same. The English demand that great officers of state be appointed by Parliament was a deliberate attempt to copy the settlement that Charles had formed with the Scots in 1641. Finally, both the Irish and English, adopting something that had been first established by the Scots, formed recess committees which sat when the main bodies of their Parliaments were not in session.

Yet the Scottish determination to alter the machinery of the English state so that a British King could never again mobilise the resources of his more powerful southern kingdom against the subjects of his northern kingdom eventually induced an equal and opposite reaction in Charles's favour. Central to the Scottish programme was the export of their Presbyterian Church, though Charles had made it clear that he would never assent to the abolition of episcopacy in England. As further reformation of the Church became indelibly associated with a breakdown in law and order there occurred a haemorrhaging of support from Pym and a growing resentment of his Scottish allies. Indeed, after an extensive examination of those who lined up behind Charles in 1642, Russell has concluded that 'the Royalist party was an anti-Scottish party before it was a Royalist party'.[12]

Not only does this British interpretation of events offer an explanation of why the King gained a party in England but it contributes towards an understanding of why the royal party and its opponents were unable to settle their differences. In the first instance, as Russell observes, this was because 'the inner ring of the Twelve Peers [having committed treason by colluding with the Scots] could not afford any settlement which gave them less than total success'.[13] Second, Charles baulked at any accommodation with those he regarded as responsible for the death of his leading minister, Strafford. Above all, resentment of Scottish interference in English affairs strengthened the position of the King, making him less inclined to offer the sorts of concession demanded by Pym and his allies.

Nevertheless, Anglo-Scottish collusion lasted long enough to ensure that Charles's surrender to the Covenanters in Scotland was total. The immediate effect of the King assenting to the Covenanter demands by signing the Treaty of London in August 1641 was that the rebels withdrew their army from England, and, in so doing, severed their alliance with the English Parliament. However, Charles was unable to benefit from these circumstances because the conjunction of events between the three kingdoms now operated in such a way as to encourage the Catholic Irish to rise in violence. This in turn introduced into English political affairs an ideological issue over which men were ultimately prepared to fight: could Charles be trusted to lead the army that all agreed must be raised in order to suppress the Irish?

It is no longer possible to perceive the Irish Rebellion of October 1641 as a random event. Instead, it should be understood as a direct consequence of decisions taken in London and Edinburgh. Anglo-Scottish collusion persuaded the Catholic Irish to fear for the demise of Catholicism, a concern which became palpable when the Petition of Twelve Peers requested Charles to effect the 'uniting of both your realms [i.e. Scotland and England] against the common enemies of the reformed religion [i.e. Ireland]'. Moreover, the Covenanters had demonstrated that rebellion could be met with reward. Indeed, the Irish rebels sought, as one of their leaders noted, 'to imitate Scotland, who got a privilege by that course [i.e. rebellion]'.[14] Yet another remarked that the Scots had taught them their 'A, B, C'.[15]

According to this analysis, it does seem as though the necessary conditions for civil war in England were very substantially brought about as a consequence of the ways in which events in Scotland and Ireland impinged upon Charles's largest kingdom. If the 'multiple kingdom' approach is ignored England might still have had a civil war but it surely would have been of a different type and very probably of another time.

Questions

1. To what extent does a knowledge of events in Scotland and Ireland in 1637–1641 help to explain the outbreak of civil war in England in 1642?
2. In what ways is the British approach insufficient to explain the crisis in England in 1642?

ANALYSIS (2): HOW WAS CHARLES I ABLE TO ASSEMBLE A ROYALIST PARTY BY THE SUMMER OF 1642?

When the Long Parliament assembled in November 1640, the majority of members were hostile to Charles I's policies over the previous decade and determined to introduce major reforms. These sentiments were widely shared in the realm at large. Yet, less than two years later, Charles had secured the support of a sizeable royalist party, and opinion was so evenly divided that it was initially unclear which side had the better chance of winning the Civil War. The growth of a royalist party between 1640 and 1642 is crucial in explaining the outbreak of war for, as John Morrill has written, 'there could be no civil war before 1642 because there was no royalist party. The origins of the English civil war are really concerned less with the rise of opposition than with the resurgence of loyalism.'[16] Similarly, Conrad Russell has argued that 'it is the English Royalists, not the English Parliamentarians, who are the peculiarity we should be attempting to explain.'[17] How was it, then, that a royalist party grew up that was strong enough to take on Parliament?

Throughout the first six or seven months of its existence, the Long Parliament presented a remarkably united front against the Crown. The vast majority of members supported a wide-ranging series of measures intended to prevent any repetition of Charles I's personal rule. The institutions that had enforced non-parliamentary government (Star Chamber, High Commission, the judicial powers of the Privy Council and the Council of the North) were abolished during the first half of 1641; the financial expedients that had sustained it (Ship Money, forest fines, knighthood fines) were declared illegal; and the advisers most closely associated with these policies were executed (Strafford), imprisoned (Archbishop Laud) or fled abroad (Secretary Windebank). Further acts stipulated that Parliament should meet at least every three years and that the Long Parliament should not be dissolved without its own consent. In all the debates on these matters, it is practically impossible to distinguish between future Parliamentarians and future royalists. These reforms were carried by large majorities, and the minority who opposed them did not necessarily become royalists in 1642. Thus, the future Parliamentarian general the Earl of Manchester defended Star Chamber, while future royalists, including Sir Edward Hyde and Viscount Falkland, led the attack on Ship Money.[18]

This high level of agreement gradually disintegrated once Parliament began to discuss religion and the future of the Church. This became evident for the very first time – and then only very briefly – on 8–9 February 1641 when the Commons debated the root-and-branch petition, submitted by the City of London, which called for the abolition of episcopacy. The Commons split down the middle, for while some members (like Nathaniel Fiennes) championed the petitioners and advocated 'further reformation' of the Church, others (such as Viscount Falkland) urged the preservation of bishops once the Laudians had been removed. This is really the first moment at which Civil War allegiances can be anticipated, for virtually all those in the first category later became Parliamentarians while nearly all those in the second ultimately sided with the King.[19]

This division of opinion became deeper and more polarised during the summer and autumn of 1641. In late May the Commons turned to debate the issue of root-and-branch reform at greater length. Intense disagreements soon arose: the more that some members demanded a fundamental overhaul of the structures and practices of the Church, including the outright abolition of bishops and the Prayer Book, the more others recoiled from such radical solutions. Reports of spontaneous outbreaks of image breaking from all over the country convinced growing numbers of gentry that the removal of episcopacy would be the thin end of a wedge leading inexorably to the collapse of the entire social hierarchy, a breakdown in public order, and the destruction of property.[20] These fears contributed powerfully to the growth of a royalist party, because the natural rallying point for such people was Charles I, who had now abandoned the Laudians and promised on 25 January 1641 to defend 'the present established government of the Church', and to 'reduce all matters of religion and government to what they were in the purest times of Queen Elizabeth's days'.[21] It was therefore to the King that men like Viscount Falkland, Sir Edward Dering or Sir Thomas Aston, who feared the wider consequences of radical religious reforms, naturally turned during the summer and autumn of that year.[22]

It was thus over the Church that the crucial disputes first emerged, but they quickly spread outwards from that issue, with the result that within royalist thought several strands became closely intertwined. First, the royalists' defence of the Church was intimately linked to a defence of the rule of law, and a growing conviction that Charles's radical critics

– such as the members of Pym's Junto – now presented a greater danger to constitutional balance and legal process than did the King. The latter's assent to the constitutional measures of the opening months of the Long Parliament only increased his credibility as a reformed character, and helped to win over those whose main objection to the policies of the personal rule had been on the grounds of their dubious legality. Royalists' defence of the Church of England was closely bound up with the fact that it was the Church 'by law established'. A second key element was a wish to preserve existing social hierarchies and structures of government, and this was undoubtedly a powerful consideration for many members of the nobility and gentry. Third, there was also, in England, growing resentment of the demands of the Scottish Covenanters, who had forged a close alliance with the more radical Puritans within Parliament and in London. Just as Charles's strongest critics felt a real sympathy with their co-religionists north of the border, so those who became royalists generally regarded the Covenanters as intrusive and subversive.[23] A defence of the Church, the law, social hierarchy and constitutional balance thus merged with anti-Scottish sentiments to foster a surge of opinion back in favour of the King. As a result, by October 1641 Charles's closest advisers, such as Sir Edward Nicholas, were increasingly optimistic that events were moving their way.[24]

This changed dramatically at the beginning of November when the first reports reached London of a Catholic rebellion in Ireland. To many within England this appeared to prove the reality of the popish plot that they had long dreaded. The fact that the rebels claimed (probably falsely) to have been acting on a commission from the King posed with acute urgency the question of whether Charles could be trusted to lead an army against the rebels. For Pym and his allies the answer had to be an emphatic 'no', and shortly afterwards Pym tabled the Grand Remonstrance, a comprehensive indictment of Charles's kingship presented in 204 clauses, none of which addressed grievances that predated 1625.[25] This polarised parliamentary opinion still further. Many, without wishing to whitewash Charles, found the Remonstrance an intolerable encroachment on the King's discretionary right to choose his own advisers and to command the armed forces, as well as a dangerous attempt to mobilise popular support against the Crown. After a heated debate in the Commons lasting over twelve hours the Remonstrance was eventually passed early on 23 November, but only by a tiny margin of 159 votes to 148. Feelings ran high, swords were drawn at one point, and the closeness of the voting showed how far opinion had polarised.

This polarisation hardened further over the months that followed. Charles firmly rejected the Remonstrance, and then, in a desperate bid to break the deadlock, attempted to arrest five of his leading critics in the Commons and one in the Lords (4 January 1642). The attempt backfired and provoked such an outcry that Charles withdrew from London. The Houses responded by passing the Militia Ordinance (5 March 1642), which claimed that in such a national emergency they had not only a right but a duty to take control of the armed forces out of Charles's hands. This only appeared to confirm royalist fears that the Houses were attempting to seize power, and throughout the opening months of 1642 there was a steady haemorrhage of royalists from both Houses to join the King at his headquarters, first at York and then at Nottingham.

Charles responded to the Militia Ordinance by issuing commissions of array, an ancient prerogative device that allowed him to raise troops on his own authority. These commissions were sent to nobility and gentry in each county known to be sympathetic to the King. Many communities soon became sharply divided between those who wished to implement the commissions and those who tried to enforce the Militia Ordinance by raising troops for Parliament. This struggle stimulated another important motive for royalism, which was a widespread and almost instinctive feeling that in such a crisis, when the monarch requested armed support, it was a matter of honour and duty to comply. This belief – although less rational than the ideas analysed above – should not be underestimated as a cause of royalist allegiance. Thus Sir Edmund Verney, the King's standard-bearer who was killed at the Battle of Edgehill in October 1642, said that 'my conscience is only concerned in honour and gratitude to follow my master'.[26] Likewise, Lord Spencer wrote to his wife from the King's headquarters in September 1642 that he would not stay there an hour longer 'were it not for gaining honour'.[27]

Such feelings exercised an almost feudal appeal to many members of the nobility and gentry, and were especially characteristic of those who took up arms for the King (what Peter Newman has called 'armed Royalists').[28] The more moderate royalists were particularly attracted by the image of constitutional balance and propriety that Charles's propagandists projected with great success during the summer of 1642. The classic expression of this moderate image was Charles's *Answer* to the Houses' *Nineteen Propositions*, drafted on the King's behalf by Sir John Culpepper and Viscount Falkland. The *Answer* presented Charles as the protector of the rule of law, public order, the established Church and constitutional balance – the very things about which most royalists were passionate. The Parliamentarians, by contrast, were portrayed as innovators whose demands directly threatened the fundamental laws and equilibrium of the constitution. These claims further reinforced the appeal of royalism and increased the numbers who rallied to Charles when he finally raised his standard against Parliament at Nottingham on 22 August.

The emergence of a royalist party in 1641–1642 thus demonstrated the success of Charles's appeal to such values as the rule of law, the Church 'by law established', the preservation of property and the maintenance of existing institutions, as well as to the deference and sense of honour that many felt towards the Crown. These attitudes commanded enough support to enable Charles to recruit a sizeable body of loyal followers. Charles's inflexibility and deep commitment to his beliefs made him an intensely divisive leader of the nation; but ironically those were precisely the qualities that made him an attractive rallying point for the royalist party. As Conrad Russell has written, 'the very lack of flexibility that made him so poor a national leader . . . made him into a party leader whose faithful knew he would stand by them'.[29]

Questions

1. How important was fear as a factor in the emergence of the royalist party?
2. Did Charles I's actions in 1640–1642 do more to help or to hinder the growth of royalism?

SOURCES

1. THE THREE KINGDOM PROBLEM

Source A: From the Petition of Twelve Peers for the summoning of a new Parliament, 28 August 1640.

[One of] the evils and dangers whereof your Majesty may be pleased to take notice . . . [is] . . . the great mischiefs which may fall upon this kingdom if the intentions which have been credibly reported, of bringing in Irish and foreign forces, shall take effect.

Source B: The deposition of Captain Winter's servant, as presented to the Long Parliament in January 1641 and as recorded in the diary of the MP Sir Simonds D'Ewes. (Captain Winter was a gentleman of Charles I's Privy Chamber.)

He confessed . . . that the French should invade England and the Irish Scotland. That Sir Phelim O'Neill [an instigator of the Irish Rebellion] was of the blood royal of Ireland. That succour was to come to them from Spain.

Source C: Proceedings in the Long Parliament on 6 February 1641 as reported in the Anonymous Diary.

Mr Treasurer Vane reported from the Lords the Scots' thanks for the £300,000, and for calling them 'brothers'.

Source D: From Clarendon's *History*. Clarendon sat in the Long Parliament until he joined the King at York in 1642. He wrote the majority of his *History* in exile, having been banished from England in 1667.

[I consider it] probable that if the kingdom [i.e. Ireland] had contained itself within their old limits of obedience and loyalty, I should never have had ... occasion to have complained of the breaches or violation of [obedience and loyalty] in this [i.e. England]. How one, which should have [been] prevented, did contribute to the other, must be too often remembered in this ensuing discourse.

Questions

1. Read Source D. Give examples of the 'breaches' and 'violation' that Clarendon probably had in mind. [4]
*2. In what ways are the concerns articulated by the authors of Source A supported by the content of Source B? [3]
3. Noting its content and the circumstances of its provenance, how useful do you consider Source A for an historian researching methods of political opposition to Charles I? [5]
4. Referring to their provenance and content and your own knowledge, how reliable do you consider Sources B and C? [5]
5. Use these Sources and your own knowledge to assess how far Clarendon was correct in his belief 'that if the kingdom [i.e. Ireland] had contained itself within their old limits of obedience and loyalty' then England would have avoided a descent into violence? Explain your answer. [8]

Worked answer

*2. *[It is useful first to paraphrase the point of view put forward in A. This makes easier the process of comparison demanded by this question.]*

The authors of Source A are fearful that the King appears to have been advised to consider 'bringing in Irish and foreign forces', a development which they believe will lead to 'great mischiefs'. Their concern will have been deepened by the deposition of Winter's servant because he alleges that his master, a reasonably high-profile royalist with access to the King, had concluded that the Irish, supported by Spain, should invade Scotland and that 'the French should invade England'.

SOURCES

2. THE FORMATION OF A ROYALIST PARTY

Source E: From Viscount Falkland's speech on Bishops, 8 February 1641, during the House of Commons' debate on the London root-and-branch petition. This petition called for the abolition of episcopacy.

We should not root up this ancient tree as dead as it appears, till we have tried whether, by this or the like lopping of the branches, the sap which was unable to feed the whole may not serve to make what is left both grow and flourish.

Source F: From Sir Thomas Aston's *Remonstrance against Presbytery* (1641).

Under pretext of reforming the Church, the true aim of such spirits is to shake off the yoke of all obedience, either to ecclesiastical, civil, common, statute or customary laws of the kingdom, and to introduce a mere arbitrary government.

Source G: From a petition which the gentry of Cornwall sent to Parliament, *c.* 1642.

That you will be pleased to continue your great respect, dutiful love, and true obedience, to our royal sovereign, by maintaining his just and no way anti-legal prerogative ... that you will be pleased to maintain and establish the ancient, fundamental and most venerable laws, order and discipline, both of our Church and Commonwealth, to continue the reverenced office ... of Bishops ... and eternise ... the divine and excellent form of common prayer.

Source H: From Charles I's *Answer to the Nineteen Propositions*, drafted by Viscount Falkland and Sir John Culpepper, 18 June 1642.

[The *Nineteen Propositions* will overturn] the ancient, equal, happy, well-poised, and never enough commended constitution of the government of this kingdom ... [and] ... be a total subversion of the fundamental laws, and that excellent constitution of this kingdom which hath made this nation so many years both famous and happy to a great degree of envy ... [This will in turn] destroy all rights and proprieties, all distinctions of families and merit, and by this means this splendid and excellently distinguished form of government end in a dark, equal chaos of confusion, and the long line of our many noble ancestors in a Jack Cade or a Wat Tyler.

Source I: From the commonplace book of the Dorset royalist Sir John Strangways.

We of the King's party do detest monopolies and Ship Money and all the grievances of the people as much as any men living: we do well know that our estates, lives and fames are preserved by the laws; and that the King is bound by his laws. We love Parliaments . . . Where is the King's fault?

Questions

1. (i) Explain the reference to 'a Jack Cade or a Wat Tyler' in Source H. [2]
   (ii) Read Source I. Comment on the significance of the phrase 'We of the King's party do detest monopolies and Ship Money'. [3]
*2. What do Sources E–G show about the relationship between royalism and a wish to defend the established Church? [5]
3. With reference to tone and content, comment on the effectiveness of Source H as royalist propaganda. [4]
4. How useful is Source I for the historian investigating the emergence of the royalist party? [4]
5. With reference to these Sources and your own knowledge, how far would you agree that 'there was an Anglican party before there was a Royalist party'? [7]

Worked answer

*2. *[Examine closely language and tone and explore possible links between defence of the established Church and support for the King.]*

Sources E–G suggest that very close links existed between a defence of the established Church and royalism. In Source E, the future royalist Viscount Falkland opposes the abolition of episcopacy and argues that more moderate reform might revive the institution and enable it to 'grow and flourish'. Although he had no wish to restore Laudianism, Falkland wished to preserve the office of bishop. In Source F, Sir Thomas Aston accuses the radicals of using Church reform as a pretext for overthrowing the rule of all kinds of laws and replacing them with 'arbitrary government'.

He thus opposed religious radicalism for itself but also for its wider social and constitutional implications. This linkage is even more explicit in Source G, in which the Cornish gentry associate a defence of the royal prerogative with protection of the existing Church. These three Sources thus suggest that an attachment to the established Church of England was a major motive for royalist allegiance, and that by pledging to defend the Church Charles encouraged the formation of a royalist party.

NOTES

1. JAMES VI AND THE ELIZABETHAN LEGACY

1 David L. Smith: *A History of the Modern British Isles, 1603–1707: The Double Crown* (Blackwell, 1998), p. 5.

2 J. E. Neale: *Queen Elizabeth I* (Cape, 1934).

3 R. B. Outhwaite: 'Dearth, the English Crown and the "Crisis of the 1590s"', in P. Clark (ed.): *The European Crisis of the 1590s* (Allen and Unwin, 1985), p. 27.

4 G. Donaldson: *Scotland, James V–James VII* (Edinburgh University Press, 1965), pp. 236–237.

5 J. A. Sharpe: *Early Modern England, a Social History 1550–1760* (Arnold, 1987), p. 13.

6 P. Williams: *The Later Tudors, England 1547–1603* (Oxford University Press, 1995), p. 383.

7 *Ibid.*

8 The terms 'Court' and 'Country' have been used by historians as a device to discuss the tug of opposite interests within the ruling orders. See P. Zagorin: *The Court and the Country* (London, 1969).

9 K. Sharpe: 'Faction at the Early Stuart Court', *History Today*, 33 (1983), p. 40.

10 J. Guy: *Tudor England* (Oxford University Press, 1988), p. 396.

11 E. R. Foster (ed.): *Proceedings in Parliament, 1610* (2 vols, Yale University Press, 1966), I, p. 6.

12 A. Foster: 'The Clerical Estate Revitalised', in K. Fincham (ed.): *The Early Stuart Church, 1603–1642* (Macmillan, 1993), p. 151.

13 M. A. R. Graves: *Elizabethan Parliaments 1559–1601* (Longman, 1996), p. 116.

14 Guy: *op. cit.*, p. 402.

15 *Ibid.*, p. 384.

16 *Ibid.*

17   R. Lockyer: *James VI and I* (Longman, 1998), p. 79.
18   From a lecture given in Cambridge in 1997.
19   Guy: *op. cit.*, p. 389.
20   *Ibid.*, pp. 455, 456.
21   Williams: *op. cit.*, p. 478.
22   *Ibid.*, p. 492.
23   A. Dures: *English Catholicism, 1558–1642* (Longman, 1983), p. 56.
24   J. E. Neale: *Elizabeth I and her Parliaments, 1584–1601* (Cape, 1953).
25   G. R. Elton: *The Tudor Constitution: Documents and Commentary* (2nd edition, Cambridge University Press, 1982), Chapter 8, and M. A. R. Graves: *Early Tudor Parliaments, 1485–1558* (Longman, 1990).
26   Graves: *op. cit.*, p. 81.
27   Jennifer M. Brown: 'Scottish Politics, 1567–1625', in A. G. R. Smith (ed.): *The Reign of James VI and I* (Macmillan, 1973), p. 39.
28   Johann P. Sommerville (ed.): *King James VI and I: Political Writings* (Cambridge University Press, 1994), p. 28.
29   John Morrill (ed.): *The Scottish National Covenant in its British Context* (Edinburgh University Press, 1990), p. 5.
30   Michael Lynch: *Scotland: A New History* (Pimlico, 1992), p. 237.
31   Sommerville (ed.): *op. cit.*, p. 74.
32   *Ibid.*, p. 75.
33   Elton (ed.): *op. cit.*, p. 13.
34   R. Pitcairn (ed.): *The Autobiography and Diary of Mr James Melvill* (Wodrow Society, 1842), p. 370.
35   Morrill (ed.): *op. cit.*, p. 7. On the Five Articles of Perth, see also below, pp. 25–26.
36   Sommerville (ed.): *op. cit.*, p. 161.
Source A: Graves: *op. cit.*, p. 116.
Source B: *Ibid.*
Source C: Williams: *op. cit.*, p. 379.
Source D: G. R. Elton: *England under the Tudors* (3rd edition, Routledge, 1991), p. 465.
Source E: Sommerville (ed.): *op. cit.*, pp. 28–29.
Source F: William K. Boyd (ed.): *Calendar of the State Papers Relating to Scotland*, VI, 1581–1583 (Edinburgh, 1910), p. 523.
Source G: W. C. Dickinson and G. Donaldson (eds): *A Source Book of Scottish History* (Thomas Nelson, 1954), III, p. 40.
Source H: Sommerville (ed.): *op. cit.*, pp. 26–27.
Source I: Robert Ashton (ed.): *James I by his Contemporaries* (Hutchinson, 1969), pp. 4–5.

2. JAMES I: RELIGION AND THE CHURCH

1   The notion that the Gunpowder Plot was engineered by Cecil has been debunked by Mark Nicholls. See Mark Nicholls: *Investigating Gunpowder Plot* (Manchester University Press, 1991).

2   Johann P. Sommerville (ed.): *King James VI and I: Political Writings* (Cambridge University Press, 1994), p. 140 (speech of 19 March 1604).

3   Kenneth Fincham and Peter Lake: 'The Ecclesiastical Policy of King James I', *Journal of British Studies*, 24 (1985), pp. 171–172.

4   *Ibid.*, p. 174.

5   S. J. Houston: *James I* (2nd edition, Longman, 1995), p. 59.

6   Roger Lockyer: *James VI and I* (Longman, 1998), p. 111.

7   Fincham and Lake: *op. cit.*, p. 179.

8   *Ibid.*, p. 184.

9   *Ibid.*, pp. 184, 185.

10 *Ibid.*, p. 186.

11 *Ibid.*

12 Patrick Collinson: *The Religion of Protestants: The Church in English Society, 1559–1625* (Oxford University Press, 1982), p. 92.

13 J. P. Kenyon (ed.): *The Stuart Constitution: Documents and Commentary* (2nd edition, Cambridge University Press, 1986), pp. 111, 115.

14 *Ibid.*, pp. 126–128.

15 *Ibid.*, p. 114.

16 Conrad Russell: *Parliaments and English Politics, 1621–1629* (Oxford University Press, 1979), p. 420.

17 John Morrill: 'A British Patriarchy? Ecclesiastical imperialism under the early Stuarts', in Anthony Fletcher and Peter Roberts (eds): *Religion, Culture and Society in Early Modern Britain: Essays in Honour of Patrick Collinson* (Cambridge University Press, 1994), pp. 209–237.

18 S. R. Gardiner: *History of England from the accession of James I to the Outbreak of the Civil War, 1603–1642* (10 vols, Longman, 1883–1884), V, p. 354.

19 John Hacket: *Scrinia Reserata: A Memorial Offer'd to the Great Deservings of John Williams, D.D.* (London, 1692), p. 64.

Source A: Kenyon (ed.): *op. cit.*, pp. 117–119.

Source B: Fincham and Lake: *op. cit.*, p. 175. James's comments were in response to John Knewstubb's request that 'some honest ministers in Suffolk' be granted a dispensation because 'it would make much against their credits in the county to be now forced to the surplice and the cross in baptism'.

Source C: Kenyon (ed.): *op. cit.*, pp. 122–123.

Source D: G. P. V. Akrigg (ed.): *Letters of King James VI and I* (University of California Press, 1984), p. 339.

Source E: Irene Carrier: *James VI and I: King of Great Britain* (Cambridge University Press, 1998), pp. 72–73.

Source F: Akrigg (ed.): *op. cit.*, p. 207.

Source G: Kenyon (ed.): *op. cit.*, p. 170.

Source H: *Ibid.*, p. 130.

Source I: Robert Ashton (ed.): *James I by his Contemporaries* (Hutchinson, 1969), pp. 197–198.

3. JAMES I: PARLIAMENTS AND FINANCES

1   C. Russell: *Parliaments and English Politics, 1621–1629* (Oxford University Press, 1979), p. 3 (hereafter *Parliaments*).

2   E. R. Foster (ed.): *Proceedings in Parliament, 1610* (2 vols, Yale University Press, 1966), I, p. 6; John Hacket: *Scrinia Reserata: A Memorial Offer'd to the Great Deservings of John Williams, D.D.* (2 vols, London, 1693), I, p. 225.

3   G. P. V. Akrigg (ed.): *Letters of King James VI and I* (University of California Press, 1984), p. 113.

4   Anne Somerset: *Unnatural Murder, Poison at the Court of James I* (Phoenix, 1998), p. 40.

5   John Guy: *Tudor England* (Oxford University Press, 1988), p. 384.

6   J. P. Kenyon (ed.): *Stuart England* (Penguin, 1978), p. 13.

7   *Journals of the House of Commons* (hereafter *CJ*), I, p. 282.

8   Maija Jansson (ed.): *Proceedings in Parliament 1614 (House of Commons)* (American Philosophical Society, 1988), pp. 423–424.

9   C. Russell: 'Parliament and the King's Finances', in C. Russell (ed.): *The Origins of the English Civil War* (Macmillan, 1973), p. 101.

10 Lawrence Stone: *The Crisis of the Aristocracy, 1558–1641* (Oxford University Press, 1965), p. 127.

11 C. Durston: *James I* (Routledge, 1993), p. 30.

12 C. Russell: 'Parliamentary History in Perspective', *History*, 61 (1976), p. 22 (hereafter, 'Perspective').

13 David L. Smith: *A History of the Modern British Isles, 1603–1707: The Double Crown* (Blackwell, 1998), p. 35.

14 Wallace Notestein: 'The Winning of the Initiative by the House of Commons', *Proceedings of the British Academy*, 11 (1924–1925), pp. 125–175. For other examples of the Whiggish interpretation see especially S. R. Gardiner: *History of England from the Accession of James I to the Outbreak of the Civil War, 1603–1642* (10 vols, Longman, 1883–1884) and G. M. Trevelyan: *England under the Stuarts* (Methuen, 1904).

15 For a useful summary of the revisionist position see Glenn Burgess:

'On Revisionism: an Analysis of Early Stuart Historiography in the 1970s and 1980s', *Historical Journal*, 33 (1990), pp. 609–627.

16 *CJ*, I, p. 171.

17 James Spedding (ed.): *The Works of Francis Bacon* (1874), X, p. 200.

18 Foster (ed.): *op. cit.*, II, p. 309.

19 J. R. Tanner (ed.): *Constitutional Documents of the Reign of James I* (Cambridge University Press, 1930), p. 279.

20 J. P. Kenyon (ed.): *The Stuart Constitution: Documents and Commentary* (2nd edition, Cambridge University Press, 1986), p. 31.

21 Tanner (ed.): *op. cit.*, p. 279.

22 Kenyon (ed.): *op. cit.*, pp. 42–43.

23 Russell: 'Perspective', p. 3.

24 For a useful summary of the arguments of those who have criticised the revisionist position see T. K. Rabb and D. Hirst: 'Revisionism Revised: Two Perspectives on Early Stuart Parliamentary History', in *Past and Present*, 92 (1981), pp. 55–99.

25 R. C. Munden: 'James I and "the growth of Mutual Distrust": King, Commons, and Reform, 1603–1604', in Kevin Sharpe (ed.): *Faction and Parliament: Essays on Early Stuart history* (Methuen, 1985), p. 57.

26 J. Wormald: 'James VI, James I and the Identity of Britain', in B. Bradshaw and J. Morrill (eds): *The British Problem, c. 1534–1707: State Formation in the Atlantic Archipelago* (Macmillan, 1996), p. 164.

27 Kenyon (ed.): *op. cit.*, p. 43.

28 Russell: 'Perspective', p. 22.

29 Russell: *Parliaments*, p. 53.

30 Russell: 'Perspective', p. 6.

31 D. Hirst: *Authority and Conflict: England 1603–1658* (Edward Arnold, 1986), p. 135.

Source A: I. Carrier: *James VI and I: King of Great Britain* (Cambridge University Press, 1998), p. 102.

Source B: *Ibid.*, p. 107.

Source C: *Ibid.*, pp. 112–113.

Source D: R. Lockyer: *James VI and I* (Longman, 1998), p. 87.

Source E: Carrier: *op. cit.*, p. 121.

Source F: *Ibid.*, p. 84.

Source G: *Ibid.*, pp. 80–81.

Source H: *Ibid.*, p. 88.

Source I: Gardiner: *op. cit.*, II, p. 251.

Source J: Carrier: *op. cit.*, p. 94.

4. BUCKINGHAM AND FOREIGN POLICY, 1618–1628

1 D. H. Willson: *King James VI and I* (Cape, 1966), pp. 384–385.
2 S. R. Gardiner: *History of England from the Accession of James I to the Outbreak of the Civil War 1603–1642* (10 vols, Longman, 1883–1884), VI, p. 358.
3 H. R. Trevor-Roper: *Archbishop Laud* (Macmillan, 1962), p. 51.
4 C. Roberts: *The Growth of Responsible Government in Stuart England* (Cambridge University Press, 1966), p. 54.
5 C. Russell: *Parliaments and English Politics 1621–1629* (Oxford University Press, 1979), p. 10.
6 R. Lockyer: *Buckingham: The life and Political Career of George Villiers, first Duke of Buckingham 1592–1628* (Longman, 1981), p. 269.
7 J. P. Kenyon (ed.): *The Stuart Constitution: Documents and Commentary* (Cambridge University Press, 1966), p. 25.
8 Russell: *op. cit.*, pp. 9, 11.
9 See especially Richard Cust and Ann Hughes (eds): *Conflict in Early Stuart England: Studies in Religion and Politics, 1603–1642* (Longman, 1989), pp. 3–4, 19–21, 140–143, 145–159, 231–240.
10 Lockyer: *op. cit.*, p. 307.
11 *Ibid.*, p. 100.
12 David L. Smith: *A History of the Modern British Isles, 1603–1707: The Double Crown* (Blackwell, 1998), p. 62.
13 *Ibid.*, p. 70.
14 *Ibid.*
15 *Ibid.*, p. 72.
16 Lockyer: *op. cit.*, p. 441.
17 *Ibid.*, p. 442.
18 Quoted in Smith: *op. cit.*, p. 67.
19 Kenyon (ed.): *op. cit.*, p. 59.
20 *Ibid.*
21 K. Sharpe: *The Personal Rule of Charles I* (Yale University Press, 1992), p. 180.
22 Kenyon (ed.): *op. cit.*, pp. 50–51.
23 Smith: *op. cit.*, p. 68.
24 J. R. Tanner (ed.): *Constitutional Documents of the Reign of James I* (Cambridge University Press, 1930), pp. 284, 289.
25 Roger Lockyer: *James VI and I* (Longman, 1998), pp. 151–152.
26 *Ibid.*, p. 152.
27 Christopher Durston: *James I* (Routledge, 1993), p. 45.
28 *Ibid.*, p. 51.
29 Anthony Weldon: *The Court and Character of King James* (London, 1650), p.189.
30 Edward Hyde, Earl of Clarendon: *The History of the Rebellion and*

Civil Wars in England, ed. W. Dunn Macray (6 vols, Clarendon Press, 1888), I, pp. 32–33 (Book I, § 51).

31 Stellionatus: someone born of a newt, thus slippery, evasive. I wish to thank Simon Cox for this reference.

32 Sejanus: the lowly born favourite of the Emperor Tiberius. He climbed the ranks through criminal behaviour and plotted to displace Tiberius. The Emperor, at last realising Sejanus' intentions, ordered his execution.

33 Tacitus: a contemporary historian of the classical period whose *Annals* were generally regarded as authoritative.

Source A: P. Gibbs: *The Romance of George Villiers* (Hutchinson, 1908), p. 221.

Source B: R. Lockyer: *Buckingham*, p. 326.

Source C: Lucy Hutchinson: *Memoirs of the Life of Colonel Hutchinson* (Everyman, 1995), pp. 67, 69.

Source D: S. J. Houston: *James I* (2nd edition, Longman, 1995), p. 130.

Source E: Irene Carrier: *James VI and I: King of Great Britain* (Cambridge University Press, 1998), p. 134.

Source F: *Ibid.*, p. 137.

Source G: *Calendar of State Papers Venetian*, XIX (1625–1626), pp. 96–97.

Source H: J. R. Dasent *et al.* (eds): *The Acts of the Privy Council of England* (46 vols, HMSO, 1890–1964), June–December 1626, p. 284.

Source I: Public Record Office: State Papers Domestic, Charles I, SP 16/78/71.

5. CHARLES I: RULE WITH PARLIAMENTS, 1625–1629

1 G. R. Elton: *Studies in Tudor and Stuart Politics and Government* (4 vols, Cambridge University Press, 1974–1992), III, pp. 3–57.

2 *Journals of the House of Lords*, III, p. 435.

3 M. F. Keeler, M. J. Cole, and W. B. Bidwell (eds): *Proceedings in Parliament, 1628* (6 vols, Yale University Press, 1977–1983), II, p. 58.

4 L. J. Reeve: 'The Legal Status of the Petition of Right', *Historical Journal*, 29 (1986), pp. 257–277; E. R. Foster: 'Printing the Petition of Right', *Huntington Library Quarterly*, 38 (1974–1975), pp. 81–83.

5 Richard Cust: *The Forced Loan and English Politics, 1626–1628* (Oxford University Press, 1987), pp. 27–36, 48–49, 87–90, 217–218, 328–329.

6 Peter Donald: *An Uncounselled King: Charles I and the Scottish Troubles, 1637–1641* (Cambridge University Press, 1990).

7 M. B. Young: *Servility and Service: The Life and Work of Sir John Coke* (Boydell and Brewer, 1986), p. 274.

8 L. J. Reeve: *Charles I and the Road to Personal Rule* (Cambridge University Press, 1989), p. 282.

9 *Ibid.*, especially chs 8 and 9.

10 Chris R. Kyle: 'Prince Charles in the Parliaments of 1621 and 1624', *Historical Journal*, 41 (1998), pp. 603–624, at p. 621.

11 Maija Jansson and W. B. Bidwell (eds): *Proceedings in Parliament, 1626* (4 vols, Yale University Press, 1991–1996), III, pp. 219, 223.

12 See above, p. 70.

13 S. R. Gardiner (ed.): *Constitutional Documents of the Puritan Revolution, 1625–1660* (3rd edition, Oxford University Press, 1906), pp. 79, 82.

14 Peter Lake: 'Anti-popery: the Structure of a Prejudice', in Richard Cust and Ann Hughes (eds): *Conflict in Early Stuart England: Studies in Religion and Politics, 1603–1642* (Longman, 1989), p. 84.

15 Edward Hyde, Earl of Clarendon: *The History of the Rebellion and Civil Wars in England*, ed. W. Dunn Macray (6 vols, Clarendon Press, 1888), I, p. 28 (Book I, § 44).

16 Michael A. R. Graves: *The Tudor Parliaments: Crown, Lords and Commons, 1485–1603* (Longman, 1985), p. 160; David L. Smith: *The Stuart Parliaments, 1603–1689* (Arnold, 1999), p. 236.

Source A: Richard Cust: 'Charles I and a Draft Declaration for the 1628 Parliament', *Historical Research*, 63 (1990), p. 160.

Source B: Gardiner (ed.): *op. cit.*, p. 69.

Source C: *Ibid.*, p. 70.

Source D: *Ibid.*, pp. 82–83.

Source E: *Ibid.*, pp. 91, 97–98.

Source F: J. F. Larkin (ed.): *Stuart Royal Proclamations: Vol. II. Royal Proclamations of King Charles I, 1625–46* (Clarendon Press, 1983), pp. 110–111.

Source G: Robert Sibthorpe: *Apostolike Obedience* (London, 1627), pp. 16–17.

Source H: J. R. Dasent et al. (eds): *The Acts of the Privy Council of England* (46 vols, HMSO, 1890–1964), January–August 1627, p. 62.

Source I: Cust: *Forced Loan*, pp. 172–174.

Source J: *Ibid.*, pp. 178–179.

6. CHARLES I: RULE WITHOUT PARLIAMENTS, 1629–1640

1 J. F. Larkin (ed.): *Stuart Royal Proclamations: Vol. II. Royal Proclamations of King Charles I, 1625–46* (Clarendon Press, 1983), p. 228.

2   S. R. Gardiner: *History of England from the Accession of James I to the Outbreak of the Civil War, 1603–1642* (10 vols, Longman, 1883–1884), VII–IX.

3   Kevin Sharpe: *The Personal Rule of Charles I* (Yale University Press, 1992).

4   Conrad Russell: *Unrevolutionary England, 1603–1642* (Hambledon Press, 1990), p. 142.

5   Kenneth Fincham: 'The Judges' Decision on Ship Money in February 1637 – the Reaction of Kent', *Bulletin of the Institute of Historical Research*, 57 (1984), p. 233.

6   Christopher Hill: 'Censorship and English Literature', in *The Collected Essays of Christopher Hill, Vol. I: Writing and Revolution in Seventeenth Century England* (Harvester Press, 1985), pp. 32–71.

7   Sharpe: *op. cit.*, pp. 644–654; John Morrill: *The Nature of the English Revolution* (Longman, 1993), pp. 280–281.

8   Edward Hyde, Earl of Clarendon: *The History of the Rebellion and Civil Wars in England*, ed. W. Dunn Macray (6 vols, Clarendon Press, 1888), I, p. 93 (Book I, § 159).

9   Morrill: *op. cit.*, p. 288.

10   R. W. K. Hinton: 'Was Charles I a Tyrant?', *The Review of Politics*, 18 (1956), pp. 86–87.

11   John Hacket: *Scrinia Reserata: A Memorial Offer'd to the Great Deservings of John Williams, D.D.* (London, 1692), p. 64.

12   Peter Lake: 'The Laudian Style', in Kenneth Fincham (ed.): *The Early Stuart Church, 1603–1642* (Macmillan, 1993), pp. 163, 183.

13   Nicholas Tyacke: *Anti-Calvinists: The Rise of English Arminianism, c. 1590–1640* (Oxford University Press, 1987), p. 269.

14   J. P. Kenyon (ed.): *The Stuart Constitution: Documents and Commentary* (2nd edition, Cambridge University Press, 1986), p. 143.

15   *Ibid.*, pp. 147–148.

16   *Ibid.*, p. 148.

17   David L. Smith: *A History of the Modern British Isles, 1603–1707: The Double Crown* (Blackwell, 1998), p. 95.

18   John Fielding: 'Opposition to the Personal Rule of Charles I: the Diary of Robert Woodford, 1637–1641', *Historical Journal*, 31 (1988), pp. 769–788 (quotations at pp. 778–779). See also Tom Webster: *Godly Clergy in Early Stuart England: The Caroline Puritan Movement, c. 1620–1643* (Cambridge University Press, 1997), pp. 217–220.

19   Ann Hughes: 'Thomas Dugard and his Circle in the 1630s – a "Parliamentary–Puritan" connexion?', *Historical Journal*, 29 (1986), pp. 771–793.

20   Webster: *op. cit.*, ch. 12.

21   *Ibid.*, ch. 15.

22 Hugh Trevor-Roper: *Catholics, Anglicans and Puritans* (Fontana Press, 1989), ch. 2; Kenneth Fincham: 'Oxford and the Early Stuart Polity', in Nicholas Tyacke (ed.): *The History of the University of Oxford, Vol. IV. Seventeenth-century Oxford* (Clarendon Press, 1997), pp. 198–210; Kevin Sharpe: 'Archbishop Laud and the University of Oxford', in Hugh Lloyd-Jones, Valerie Pearl and Blair Worden (eds): *History and Imagination: Essays in Honour of H. R. Trevor-Roper* (Duckworth, 1981), pp. 146–164.

23 Sharpe: *Personal Rule*, pp. 383–392.

24 Judith Maltby (ed.): 'Petitions for Episcopacy and the Book of Common Prayer on the Eve of the Civil War 1641–1642', in Stephen Taylor (ed.): *From Cranmer to Davidson: A Church of England Miscellany* (Church of England Record Society, 7, 1999), pp. 140–141, 158–159, 159–160, 161; Judith Maltby: *Prayer Book and People in Elizabethan and Early Stuart England* (Cambridge University Press, 1998), pp. 126–128.

Source A: Smith: *op. cit.*, p. 84.

Source B: Christopher W. Daniels and John Morrill: *Charles I* (Cambridge University Press, 1988), pp. 44–46.

Source C: *Ibid.*, p. 47.

Source D: Larkin (ed.): *op. cit.*, II, p. 467.

Source E: *Calendar of State Papers Venetian*, XIX (1625–1626), p. 21.

Source F: W. Scott (ed.): *The Works of William Laud* (7 vols, Clarendon Press, 1847–1860), II, p. xvi.

Source G: *Ibid.*, II, p. 152.

Source H: *Ibid.*, VI, p. 57.

Source I: *Ibid.*, III, pp. 407, 411.

Source J: *The Letany of John Bastwick* (London, 1637), pp. 4–6, 17.

7. IRELAND UNDER SIR THOMAS WENTWORTH, EARL OF STRAFFORD

1 S. R. Gardiner: 'Sir Thomas Wentworth, First Earl of Strafford', in Leslie Stephen and Sidney Lee (eds): *The Dictionary of National Biography* (63 vols, London, 1885–1900), LX, pp. 268–283, at p. 270.

2 J. P. Kenyon (ed.): *The Stuart Constitution: Documents and Commentary* (2nd edition, Cambridge University Press, 1986), p. 191.

3 W. A. H. Gardner, Lady Burghlere: *Strafford* (2 vols, London, 1931); C. V. Wedgwood: *Strafford 1593–1641* (Cape, 1935); and F. W. F. Smith, Earl of Birkenhead: *Strafford* (London, 1938).

4 T. Ranger: 'Strafford in Ireland, a Revaluation', in T. Aston (ed.): *Crisis in Europe 1560–1660* (Routledge, 1966), p. 272.

5   Wedgwood: *op. cit.*, pp. 346–347.
6   H. Kearney: *Strafford in Ireland 1633–1641: A Study in Absolutism* (Cambridge University Press, 1989), pp. 153 and 218.
7   Ranger: *op. cit.*, p. 293.
8   J. F. Merritt, 'The Historical Reputation of Thomas Wentworth', in J. F. Merritt (ed.): *The Political World of Thomas Wentworth, Earl of Strafford 1621–1641* (Cambridge University Press, 1996), p. 22.
9   William Knowler (ed.): *The Earl of Strafford's Letters and Dispatches* (2 vols, London, 1739), I, p. 199.
10 Kearney, *op. cit.*, p. 54.
11 A. Clarke: *The Old English in Ireland 1625–1642* (Trinity Press, 1966), pp. 238–254.
12 C. V. Wedgwood: *Thomas Wentworth, First Earl of Strafford 1593–1641* (Jonathan Cape, 1961), p. 156.
13 *Ibid.*, p. 157.
14 *Ibid.*, p. 169.
15 Wardship was the monarch's feudal right to assume the guardianship of those of its tenants-in-chief who inherited estates as minors. This right was either administered to the Crown through the Court of Wards or sold off directly to interested parties.
16 Kearney: *op. cit.*, p. 80.
17 Historical Manuscripts Commission, *Manuscripts in Various Collections* (London, 1914), VII, p. 410.
18 Knowler (ed.): *op. cit.*, I, pp. 258, 339.
19 *Ibid.*, I, p. 450.
20 Wedgwood: *Thomas Wentworth*, p. 176.
21 *Ibid.*, p. 179.
22 Kearney: *op. cit.*, p. 113.
23 Knowler (ed.): *op. cit.*, II, p. 33.
24 Clarke: *op. cit.*, p. 97.
25 Sir Richard Fanshawe: 'The Fall', in A. Fowler (ed.): *The New Oxford Book of Seventeenth-century Verse* (Oxford University Press, 1992), p. 404.
Source A: John H. Timmis III: *Thine is the Kingdom: The Trial of Strafford* (University of Alabama Press, 1974), p. 19.
Source B: Wedgwood: *Thomas Wentworth*, p. 164.
Source C: Kenyon (ed.): *op. cit.*, p. 434.
Source D: Timmis, *op. cit.*, p. 77.
Source E: *Ibid.*, pp. 138–139.
Source F: *Ibid.*, p. 143.
Source G: Edward Hyde, Earl of Clarendon: *The History of the Rebellion and Civil Wars in England*, ed. W. Dunn Macray (6 vols, Clarendon Press, 1888), I, p. 337 (Book III, § 197).

8. THE COMING OF CIVIL WAR

1   C. Russell: *The Crisis of Parliaments: English History: 1509–1660* (Oxford University Press, 1971), p. 310.

2   C. Russell: *The Causes of the English Civil War* (Oxford University Press, 1990), p. 27; J. H. Elliott: 'A Europe of Composite Monarchies', *Past and Present*, 137 (November 1992), pp. 48–71.

3   Ann Hughes: *The Causes of the English Civil War* (Macmillan, 1992), pp. 58–59.

4   J. Morrill: *The Nature of the English Revolution* (Longman, 1993), pp. 262, 259.

5   Russell: *Causes*, pp. 23–24.

6   C. Russell: *The Fall of the British Monarchies, 1637–1642* (Oxford University Press, 1991), pp. 61–62.

7   M. Perceval-Maxwell: *The Outbreak of the Irish Rebellion of 1641* (Gill and Macmillan, 1994), p. 43.

8   K. Sharpe: *The Personal Rule of Charles I* (Yale University Press, 1992), p. 823.

9   P. H. Donald: 'New light on the Anglo-Scottish contacts of 1640', *Historical Research*, 62 (1989), p. 222.

10 S. R. Gardiner (ed.): *The Constitutional Documents of the Puritan Revolution, 1625–1660* (3rd edition, Oxford University Press, 1906), pp. 134–136.

11 A. Fletcher: *The Outbreak of the English Civil War* (Arnold, 1981), pp. 12, 14.

12 Russell: *Causes*, p. 15.

13 Russell: *Fall*, p. 153.

14 C. Russell: 'The British Problem and the English Civil War', in C. Russell: *Unrevolutionary England, 1603–1642* (Hambledon Press, 1990), p. 243.

15 M. Perceval-Maxwell: 'Ulster 1641 in the Context of Political Developments in the Three Kingdoms', in Brian MacCuarta (ed.): *Ulster 1641* (Institute of Irish Studies, 1997), p. 106.

16 John Morrill: *Revolt in the Provinces: The People of England and the Tragedies of War, 1630–1648* (2nd edition, Longman, 1999), p. 24.

17 Russell: *Fall*, p. 526.

18 David L. Smith: *Constitutional Royalism and the Search for Settlement, c. 1640–1649* (Cambridge University Press, 1994), pp. 69–71.

19 *Ibid.*, pp. 71–73.

20 Morrill: *Revolt in the Provinces*, pp. 47–74.

21 J. P. Kenyon (ed.): *The Stuart Constitution: Documents and Commentary* (2nd edition, Cambridge University Press, 1986), p. 17.

22 Derek Hirst: 'The Defection of Sir Edward Dering, 1640–1641',

Historical Journal, 15 (1972), pp. 193–208; Judith Maltby, *Prayer Book and People in Elizabethan and Early Stuart England* (Cambridge University Press, 1998), especially pp. 130–180.

23 A colourful example of such views is found in a letter of 1639 written by Thomas Windebank (the Secretary's son) which referred to 'those scurvy, filthy, dirty, nasty, lousy, itchy, scabby, shitten, stinking, slovenly, snotty-nosed, logger-headed, foolish, insolent, proud, beggarly, impertinent, absurd, grout-headed, villainous, barbarous, bestial, false, lying, roguish, devilish, long-eared, short-haired, damnable, atheistical, puritanical crew of the Scottish Covenant' (Russell: *Causes*, p. 13).

24 Russell: *Unrevolutionary England*, pp. 263–264.

25 Gardiner (ed.): *op. cit.*, pp. 202–232. The King's answer is at pp. 233–236.

26 Edward Hyde, Earl of Clarendon: *The Life of Edward, Earl of Clarendon . . . Written by Himself* (3 vols, Clarendon Press, 1827), I, p. 160.

27 Smith: *op. cit.*, p. 210.

28 P. R. Newman: *The Old Service: Royalist Regimental Colonels and the Civil War, 1642–1646* (Manchester University Press, 1993); P. R. Newman: 'The King's Servants: Conscience, Principle, and Sacrifice in Armed Royalism', in John Morrill, Paul Slack and Daniel Woolf (eds): *Public Duty and Private Conscience in Seventeenth-century England: Essays presented to G. E. Aylmer* (Oxford University Press, 1993), pp. 225–241.

29 Russell: *Causes*, p. 210.

Source A: Gardiner (ed.): *op. cit.*, pp. 134–136.

Source B: W. H. Coates, A. S. Young and V. F. Snow (eds): *The Private Journals of the Long Parliament, 3 January to 5 March 1642* (Yale University Press, 1982), p. 3.

Source C: M. Jansson (ed.): *Two Diaries of the Long Parliament* (Alan Sutton, 1984), p. 83.

Source D: Edward Hyde, Earl of Clarendon: *The History of the Rebellion and Civil Wars in England*, ed. W. Dunn Macray (6 vols, Clarendon Press, 1888), I, p. 412 (Book IV, § 42).

Source E: Smith: *op. cit.*, p. 72.

Source F: Morrill: *Revolt in the Provinces*, p. 71.

Source G: Judith Maltby (ed.): 'Petitions for Episcopacy and the Book of Common Prayer on the Eve of the Civil War', in Stephen Taylor (ed.): *From Cranmer to Davidson: A Miscellany* (Church of England Record Society, 1999), VII, p. 147.

Source H: John Rushworth: *Historical Collections of Private Passages of State* (8 vols, London, 1680–1701), IV, pp. 725–735.

Source I: Beinecke Library, Yale University: Osborn MS b. 304 (commonplace book of Sir John Strangways), p. 47.

SELECT BIBLIOGRAPHY

PRIMARY SOURCES

A comprehensive collection of primary material can be found in J. P. Kenyon (ed.): *The Stuart Constitution* (2nd edition, Cambridge University Press, 1986). Varied selections of extracts relating to the first two Stuart Kings of England can be found in Irene Carrier: *James VI and I: King of Great Britain* (Cambridge University Press, 1998), and Christopher W. Daniels and John Morrill: *Charles I* (Cambridge University Press, 1988). Ann Hughes: *Seventeenth-century England: A Changing Culture*, vol. 1 (Ward Lock, 1980) contains interesting documents relating to political, religious and social themes. David Cressy and Lori Anne Ferrell (eds): *Religion and Society in Early Modern England: A Sourcebook* (Routledge, 1996) is very useful on the Church, while for political ideas David Wootton (ed.): *Divine Right and Democracy* (Penguin, 1986) offers an excellent anthology.

SECONDARY SOURCES

The following books provide useful overviews of the period as a whole: David L. Smith: *A History of the Modern British Isles: The Double Crown, 1603–1707* (Blackwell, 1998); Graham E. Seel: *Regicide and Republic, England 1603–1660* (Cambridge University Press, 2001). Barry Coward: *The Stuart Age: England, 1603–1714* (2nd edition, Longman, 1994); Mark Kishlansky: *A Monarchy Transformed: Britain, 1603–1714* (Penguin, 1996); A. G. R. Smith: *The Emergence of a Nation*

State: The Commonwealth of England, 1529–1660 (2nd edition, Longman, 1997); and Roger Lockyer: *The Early Stuarts: A Political History of England, 1603–1642* (2nd edition, Longman, 1999). Also very valuable, but requiring slightly more prior knowledge of the period, are Derek Hirst: *England in Conflict, 1603–1660: Kingdom, Community, Commonwealth* (Arnold, 1999), and Jonathan Scott: *England's Troubles: Seventeenth-century English Political Instability in European Context* (Cambridge University Press, 2000). The thematic essays in John Morrill (ed.): *The Oxford Illustrated History of Tudor and Stuart Britain* (Oxford University Press, 1996) are very stimulating and helpful.

There are excellent thematic discussions of the causes of the English Civil War in Norah Carlin: *The Causes of the English Civil War* (Blackwell, 1999); Ann Hughes: *The Causes of the English Civil War* (2nd edition, Macmillan, 1998); and Conrad Russell: *The Causes of the English Civil War* (Oxford University Press, 1990). Two interesting collections of essays on pre-Civil War England are Howard Tomlinson (ed.): *Before the English Civil War* (Macmillan, 1983), and Richard Cust and Ann Hughes (eds): *Conflict in Early Stuart England: Studies in Religion and Politics, 1603–1642* (Longman, 1989).

For the history of early Stuart Parliaments, see David L. Smith: *The Stuart Parliaments, 1603–1689* (Arnold, 1999), and Conrad Russell: *Parliaments and English Politics, 1621–1629* (Oxford University Press, 1979). Religious developments in these years are discussed in S. Doran and C. Durston: *Princes, Pastors and People: The Church and Religion in England, 1529–1689* (Routledge, 1991), and Andrew Foster: *The Church of England, 1570–1640* (Longman, 1994). Two helpful and complementary introductions to early seventeenth-century political thought are Glenn Burgess: *The Politics of the Ancient Constitution: An Introduction to English Political Thought, 1603–1642* (Macmillan, 1992), and J. P. Sommerville: *Royalists and Patriots: Politics and Ideology in England, 1603–1640* (2nd edition, Longman, 1999).

For good, short introductions to James I's character and reign, see Christopher Durston: *James I* (Routledge, 1993), and S. J. Houston: *James I* (2nd edition, Longman, 1995). Fuller studies are found in Roger Lockyer: *James VI and I* (Longman, 1998), and Maurice Lee: *Great Britain's Solomon: James VI and I in his Three Kingdoms* (University of Illinois Press, 1990). On

Charles I, Christopher Durston: *Charles I* (Routledge, 1998), and Brian Quintrell: *Charles I, 1625–1640* (Longman, 1993) provide helpful overviews, while more extended treatments are available in Michael B. Young: *Charles I* (Macmillan, 1997), Charles Carlton: *Charles I: The Personal Monarch* (2nd edition, Routledge, 1995), and Kevin Sharpe: *The Personal Rule of Charles I* (Yale University Press, 1992).

The drift into civil war between 1638 and 1642 is charted in detail in Conrad Russell: *The Fall of the British Monarchies, 1637–1642* (Oxford University Press, 1991), and Anthony Fletcher: *The Outbreak of the English Civil War* (Arnold, 1981). John Morrill: *Revolt in the Provinces: The People of England and the Tragedies of War, 1630–1648* (2nd edition, Longman, 1999) analyses developments in the provinces, and his *The Nature of the English Revolution* (Longman, 1993) contains many important essays. Also helpful are Peter Gaunt: *The British Wars, 1637–1651* (Routledge, 1997) and Martyn Bennett: *The Civil Wars in Britain and Ireland, 1638–1651* (Blackwell, 1997).

The recent surge of work on the 'British problem' is best approached through two important collections of essays: Steven G. Ellis and Sarah Barber (eds): *Conquest and Union: Fashioning a British State 1485–1725* (Longman, 1995); and Brendan Bradshaw and John Morrill (eds): *The British Problem, c. 1534–1707: State Formation in the Atlantic Archipelago* (Macmillan, 1996). The most accessible introduction to Scottish history is Michael Lynch: *Scotland: A New History* (Pimlico, 1991), while for events in Ireland see R. F. Foster: *Modern Ireland, 1600–1972* (Penguin, 1988).

Many of the works listed above touch on English foreign policy during this period, but the most useful synthesis on that subject remains J. R. Jones: *Britain and Europe in the Seventeenth Century* (Arnold, 1966). See also Simon Adams's essay in Tomlinson (ed.): *Before the English Civil War*, noted above.

INDEX

Prayer Book 6, 18, 23, 117
Prayer Book Rebellion (1637) 82, 111, 112
Presbyterians 6–7, 12, 20
press censorship 85–6
Privy Council 3, 6, 7, 23, 70, 74, 78, 82, 84–5
Protestants 6–7, 24–5, 26, 56, 60; in Ireland 101, 103–5
Protestations 42, 68, 74, 77, 114
Prynne, William 84, 88, 95
Puritans 7, 18, 19, 21, 22–3, 24, 26, 28–30, 74, 118
Pym, John 24, 99, 114, 118; speech by 107

Raleigh, Sir Walter 5, 35
Ranger, T. 100
Religion, creation of middle way 6, 20–3; Directions to Preachers 19, 30–1; setbacks to policies 26; success of Jacobean policy 23–7, see also Church of England
Richelieu, Duc de 52, 59
Rochester, Thomas Overbury, Viscount 35
Rolle, John 54
royal prerogative 33, 39–43, 46
Royalist party 114; assembling of 116–20; emergence of 116–20
Rubens, Peter Paul 61
Rudyerd, Sir Benjamin 70, 72, 80
Russell, C. 33, 37, 38, 41, 42, 49, 111, 112, 116
Rutland, Francis Manners, Earl of 53

Salisbury, Earl of see Cecil, Robert, Earl of Salisbury
Salmacida Spolia (Webb) 93, 94
Sandys, Sir Edwin 38
Saville, Sir John 50
Saye, William Fiennes, Lord 71, 113
Scotland 5, 6, 111–12, 113
Scott, Thomas 79
Scottish National Covenant (1638) 114
Second Bishops' War (1640) 37, 99, 113
Second Book of Discipline (1578) 11
Sharpe, J.A. 2

Sharpe, K. 82, 84, 94
Ship Money 3, 81–2, 83, 94, 116, 117
Shirley, Sir Thomas 4
Short Parliament (April–May 1640) 99, 110, 112
Sibthorpe, Robert 74, 78
Somerset, Earl of see Carr, Robert, Earl of Somerset
Soubise, Duc de 59
Southampton, Thomas Wriothesley, Earl of 50
Spain 58, 81; war against 49, 51, 52, 59, 67
Spencer, Lord 119
Star Chamber 84, 89, 97, 116
Stevenson, D. 111
Stewart, Esme, Duke of Lennox 9
Stone, L. 37
Strafford, Earl of see Wentworth, Thomas, Earl of Strafford
Strangways, Sir John 123
Susa, Treaty of (1629) 60, 81
Sutcliffe, Matthew 4
Synod of Dort (1619) 19

taxation 55, 68–9, 81–2, 83; increase in/resistance to 2–3; and subsidy assessment 4–5
Third Bishops' War, possibility of 114
Thirty Years War 19, 57
Thirty-Nine Articles and Canons 103
trade 2, 38
Travers, Walter 6
Trevor-Roper, H.R. 49
Triennial Act (1641) 114
The True Law of Free Monarchies (James I) 8

Union, Act of 39
Ussher, James, Archbishop of Armagh 103

Valentine, Benjamin 68
Van Dyck, Sir Anthony 85
Verney, Sir Edmund 119

Walsingham, Sir Francis, letter from Bowes 15
wardships 37
Warwick Castle 89